Items should be returned on or before the date shown below. Items
not already requested by other borrowers may be renewed in person,
in writing or by telephone. To renew, please quote the number on the
barcode label. To renew online a PIN is required. This can be requested
at your local library.
Renew online @ **www.dublincitypubliclibraries.ie**
Fines charged for overdue items will include postage incurred in recovery.
Damage to or loss of items will be charged to the borrower.

Comhairle Cathrach
Bhaile Átha Cliath
Dublin City Council

Leaeharlanna Poiblí
Chathair Bhaile Átha
Cliath

Due Date	Due Date	Due Date

FOR THE LOVE OF
IRELAND

A COMPANION

An Hachette UK Company
www.hachette.co.uk

Summersdale Publishers Ltd
Part of Octopus Publishing Group Limited
Carmelite House
50 Victoria Embankment
LONDON
EC4Y 0DZ
UK

www.summersdale.com

Printed and bound in the Czech Republic

ISBN: 978-1-78685-051-5

Substantial discounts on bulk quantities of Summersdale books are available to corporations, professional associations and other organisations. For details contact general enquiries: telephone: +44 (0) 1243 771107, or email: enquiries@summersdale.com.

FOR THE LOVE OF
IRELAND

A COMPANION

BAIRBRE MEADE

summersdale

CONTENTS

INTRODUCTION

The Irish are known all over the world for their cheer, love of banter (and the drink), works of literature and national saint who yearly provides people the world over with the excuse for having a good time. That's not bad for such a small island clinging to the west of Europe. For much of history they have been the underdogs, though in the face of countless invasions they never gave up and always rebuilt their communities. This pattern changed in the twentieth century: Ireland as a nation was split in the 1920s and while the majority of the island is a republic, six counties in the north remain part of the United Kingdom. This book was written with the intention of giving an overview of the whole island of Ireland. It can be dipped into for information on a chosen topic or read from cover to cover as a starting point for learning about this small nation famous for Guinness and craic – and so much more.

The first three chapters go through the history of Ireland – from prehistoric times until the twentieth century – and the next chapter takes us up to the modern day. Throughout the book, we delve into a little detail on each of the four provinces of Ireland: Ulster, Munster, Leinster and Connacht. These 'portraits of a province' contain specifics about each county. The Language chapter looks at the languages spoken in Ireland, while the following one explores the celebrations we hold and festivals we enjoy. As Ireland is a nation known for its love of a good time, this chapter is full of things to do. The chapter about religion gives an overview of the different faiths within Ireland and, following from that topic, the next chapter looks at the country's previous beliefs through myths and legends. The chapters about the arts and sports describe the pastimes of Ireland and its achievements in those fields. The Science and Technology chapter follows from this, looking at our successes in science and technology, and the final chapter looks at some of our best loved dishes.

I grew up in Ireland – I have lived in Leinster, Munster and Connacht – and since then have moved to Sweden, Scotland, the US and Canada, before finally settling in England. Years of explaining my accent and my religion (or lack of), telling stories, writing about my culture and often conforming to (or confirming) the stereotype as a friendly cheerful woman who likes a drink meant that talking about my heritage, enjoying my culture and celebrating our achievements has felt like a privilege – and something I am very happy to share with you.

TIMELINE

TIMELINE

*c.*3500 BC	Farming using wall-enclosed fields.
3200 BC	Newgrange built.
*c.*AD 220	Cormac mac Airt is High King of Ireland. It is still unknown if he is legend or really part of history.
433	The first Christian bishop – Palladius – arrives in Ireland.
432	St Patrick returns to Ireland to spread Christianity.
795	Viking raids begin.
852	Dublin is established by the Vikings, Ivar Beinlaus and Olaf the White.
980	The Viking king of Dublin abdicates.

1014   The Battle of Clontarf: though Brian Boru is killed, his army is victorious and achieves the end of Viking power in Ireland.

1167   Dermot MacMurrough, king of Leinster, asks for help from England to protect his land and invites the Norman invasion.

1171   Henry II declares himself 'Lord of Ireland'.

1264   The first Irish Parliament meets, but it's only attended by prelates and magnates.

1297   First full parliament meets.

1315   Edward Bruce from Scotland arrives in Ireland to claim the high kingship and turn the Irish lords against the Anglo-Norman peers, only to be defeated and killed at the Battle of Faughart 1318.

1494   Poynings' Law curtails the power of the Irish Parliament, so that it can no longer pass a law without prior consent from the English Parliament.

1542   The Irish Parliament establishes the Kingdom of Ireland to be ruled by Henry VIII and his successors.

1594   The Nine Years' War begins when Hugh O'Neill and Red Hugh O'Donnell declare they no longer recognise Elizabeth I's rule over Ulster.

1607   The Flight of the Earls: Hugh O'Neill, Rory O'Donnell and many other earls, following their defeat, flee Ireland in fear for their safety.

1609   The Plantation of Ulster begins in earnest, as many Scottish Presbyterians settle in Northern Ireland on lands confiscated from the Irish chiefs.

1641   Another Irish rebellion, as Irish Catholic lords pit themselves against Scottish Protestant settlers.

1642   The Irish Confederate Wars begin when the Irish gentry create a confederation that rules Catholic Ireland. They support the Royalists in the English Civil War. Victory for Parliament results in a massive transfer of land in Ireland from Catholic to Protestant control.

1760   The French invade during the Seven Years' War. They take over the town and castle of Carrickfergus for five days before retreating.

1782   Poynings' Law is repealed.

1796   The French again attempt to invade Ireland, with a large force, to aid the Society of United Irishmen in overthrowing English rule but are rebuffed, mainly by winter storms.

1798   The Irish Rebellion, aided by the French. The first United Irishmen rebellion leads to the Republic of Connacht being declared at Castlebar.

1800   The Act of Union 1800 is passed formally, dissolving the Irish Parliament and creating the United Kingdom of Great Britain and Ireland.

1803   The second United Irishmen rebellion – or 'Robert Emmet's rebellion', after the student leader who led this disastrous failed uprising.

1829   Catholic Emancipation is passed, allowing Catholics to sit in Parliament.

1834   Dublin and Kingstown Railway opens – it is the first commercial railway in Ireland.

1845–1849   The Great Irish Famine. Potato blight leads to one million deaths and one million people emigrating.

1867   The Fenian Rising: the Irish Republican Brotherhood stage a rebellion.

1914   The British Parliament passes an Act that gives the Irish Home Rule, though it is simultaneously postponed for the duration of World War One.

1916   The Easter Rising: the Republic of Ireland is declared after a large-scale rising organised by the Irish Republican Brotherhood.

1918   The general election gives hard-line republican party Sinn Féin the vast majority of Westminster seats in Ireland but they refuse to take them.

1919   The first Dáil of an independent Ireland meets and issues a declaration of independence. The Irish War of Independence begins.

1921	The Irish Free State and Northern Ireland are established after the signing of the Anglo-Irish Treaty. The Irish Civil War begins.
1923	The Irish Civil War ends.
1937	A new Constitution of Ireland is adopted, ending the dominion status of the Irish Free State.
1949	The Republic of Ireland Act abolishes the remaining roles of the British monarchy in the government of the Irish State.
1955	Ireland joins the United Nations.
1969	The Troubles begin in Northern Ireland.
1973	Ireland joins the European Community and the Northern Ireland Assembly is elected.
1985	Ireland and the United Kingdom sign the Anglo-Irish Agreement.
1990	Mary Robinson is voted first female president of Ireland.
1995	The Celtic Tiger begins in Ireland, marking a time of great economic growth for the country.
1998	The Belfast Agreement is signed and a Northern Irish Assembly is set up.
1999	Ireland adopts the euro as its currency.

2008 Taoiseach Bertie Ahern resigns, in the wake of the Mahon Tribunal's investigations into allegations of financial corruption in Irish politics.

2011 The ongoing financial crisis drives Ireland into a recession, causing renewed emigration. A general election elects the thirty-first Dáil and economic recovery commences.

2015 Same-sex marriage is legalised.

HISTORY (6000 BC- ELEVENTH CENTURY)

PREHISTORIC ERA

Ireland had its first settlers in *c*.6000 BC, making it the last part of Europe to be inhabited. As the first settlers made their way across the Continent following large game animals, once the ice had melted and highland areas became filled with dense forest, Europe's population grew but Ireland remained uninhabited. Around 10,000 BC archaeologists have established the presence of huge quantities of deer but no people. By 6000 BC Ireland had become an island, blocked off by the rising sea levels from the melting ice, and migrants started arriving in search of food. They travelled over the sea and led nomadic lifestyles along the coasts, rivers and lakes, living off birds and fish. Through archaeological discoveries we have learnt something of the lifestyle of these first settlers but we have no knowledge of their beliefs, customs or society.

DID YOU KNOW?

Early settlers created areas with young shoots to attract young deer so they could ambush them. These were the first type of traps, though not in the conventional way we think of them now.

FIRST FARMERS AND THE STONE AGE

The first farmers arrived in Ireland *c.*3000 BC (farming having begun in the Middle East thousands of years before), bringing crops, domesticated animals and new methods of providing for their community. The animals were used for their meat, hides and milk. These new farmers also brought the skills to make baskets and pottery, and they knew how to polish to make tools more effective. They felled trees, clearing the impenetrable woodland and making more of the country accessible. Since jewellery made from beads, bone, stone and lignite has been found, we know that they also took pride in their appearance. Unaware of how to fertilise the soil, they would move once the land's nutrients were used up. These settlers traded with each other and even further afield than Ireland. Axes and stone were imported from various areas within and outside of the island. We know virtually nothing of their religion, though we do know that they honoured their dead. Large monuments, or Courtcairns (more commonly known as megalithic tombs or dolmens), have survived and show us that they buried their dead with items such as pottery, beads and tools. The space inside the Courtcairns suggests that ceremonies must have been performed at these passage graves. It is likely that they worshipped the sun, as many of the entrances to these monuments face the rising sun and have very precise alignment with an equinox.

BRONZE AGE

There was possibly another migration to Ireland, though it cannot now be proven, and in 2000–1200 BC metalwork arrived. Copper, which was mined throughout Ireland, and iron – from Iberia (modern-day Spain) – were combined to create bronze. This is a strong metal that was used to make utensils, ornaments, weaponry and musical instruments. Bronze was more expensive than stone, so flint was still widely used for most tools. Ireland also had gold, particularly in Co. Wicklow, but that is too soft a metal for practical tools, so it was used for decoration, particularly jewellery. These craftsmen created lunulae: crescent-shaped necklaces that have been found throughout Ireland, Britain and the Continent. Torcs (a twisted gold necklace), gorgets (much like a lunula but wider and thicker) and several other forms of decorative attire have been discovered and dated to this era.

In this early Bronze Age a new burial style was used: people were buried in single graves. Excavations have found that each of them contained a pot, some accompanying the body and presumed to have contained food. Other corpses were cremated and the remains placed in these pots. Circles of standing stones were erected, and evidence of food and vessels has been found at these sites, hinting at the fact that ceremonies were held there – they were sites of ritual.

By 800 BC new tools were found in Ireland. Ploughs pulled by oxen have been discovered and there are many more examples of jewellery. These indicate increasingly affluent settlers. The houses were largely wattle and daub but there were also crannogs, where the wealthy lived. A crannog was a man-made fortified island. This style of home lasted beyond the Bronze Age, into the Iron Age.

NEWGRANGE

Newgrange in County Meath dates from 3200 BC. It is one of the finest examples of passage tombs in the world, older than both Stonehenge and the Egyptian pyramids. More recently, it has been classified as an 'Ancient Temple', as it is believed to be a place of astrological, sacred, spiritual and ceremonial importance. The unassuming mound of grass has a white stone wall around its entrance and is roughly an acre in size. Inside, a passage leads into a chamber with three alcoves. During the winter solstice the passage and chamber are lit up perfectly by the rising sun. Surrounding the mound are 97 large stones: many are decorated, though a lot of these have been weathered over the millennia. The entrance stone remains beautifully decorated. Two other sites nearby, Knowth and Dowth, have also been designated World Heritage Sites by UNESCO.

DID YOU KNOW?

Attending the winter solstice at Newgrange is so popular that bookings are no longer accepted (people used to book years in advance) and it is now a lottery system. There is another lottery as to whether the weather will hold, since clouds invariably block out the rising sun!

CHRISTIANITY ARRIVES

The first Christians arrived in Ireland *c.*AD 400. We don't know how they integrated into society but slowly they began to influence the laws and people of the country. Though there is an inclination to believe that Ireland was shut off from its neighbours as a small island, there is ample proof to the contrary. There was plenty of trading between Ireland, Britain and Europe at this time, including items such as strong wine, oil and grain between southern Ireland and Roman traders. Archaeologists have found Roman coins in various coastal digs (though never any inland). Ireland also had an active raiders' industry both on land and at sea, with acts of piracy. St Patrick, as he recorded in his *Confession*, was abducted in his youth, brought to Ireland as a slave and subsequently escaped back to Britain. In AD 432 he returned and began to convert the people of Ireland to Christianity. St Patrick focused his attentions on the wealthy, thus ensuring that the lower-ranking society members had to convert to the same religion as their *tuath* (tribe). Throughout the fourth century the Irish fought in skirmishes and raids in nearby Britain, Spain, France and even as far as Iceland. During this time Christians preached across Ireland and converted many. They influenced changes in the law and society but the belief system became a hybrid of Christian and Celtic. Poets still travelled the country and would perform in monasteries, including at enclosed orders, where they were allowed entry and treated as important guests. Native Irish law, known as Brehon law, still prevailed; the Church originally had a ban on Christians seeking advice from Brehon lawyers but by the seventh century this slackened. Many Brehon lawyers, at this point, had been converted and there was a crossover between the secular and ecclesiastical courts.

FAMOUS FIGURES
ST PALLADIUS (FIRST CENTURYad)

The first missionary, St Palladius, was recorded by St Prosper in AD 433. Sent to Ireland by Pope Celestine I, St Palladius's attempts to convert the Irish were met with resistance, including being banished by the king of Leinster. Some records say he left Ireland for Scotland, others that he returned to Rome, but all agree that he had little success and died shortly after leaving Ireland.

FAMOUS FIGURES
NIALL OF THE NINE HOSTAGES
(c. FOURTH/FIFTH CENTURY ad)

Niall of the Nine Hostages is believed to have been a real person, though the stories are legend (see p.159 for more on the myth of Niall), as they give him unlikely powers and lifespan. As a king, he gained power within Ireland but he also fought outside of its borders, and all sources agree that he died in a battle away from Ireland, though there is no consensus on whether that happened in Britain or on the Continent. Niall was a successful warrior whose nickname derives from his ability to bring back slaves – one of those believed to be St Patrick – from his skirmishes.

CELTS

Early records of the Celts' arrival are sparse, though we know the date to be close to 500 BC. Many of our first records of Irish Celtic society come from the accounts of the Christian missionaries who sent reports of Irish culture back to Rome. We have no way of knowing if the Celts arrived as migrants or as an invading force but items excavated from this era include war trumpets, scabbards, swords and shields (thus pointing to the latter option). Having said that, the Celts were made up of many tribes, constantly warring with each other, so it is unlikely they would have had an organised invasion. By the fifth century Ireland was entirely Celtic and speaking the Irish language: Celtic gods were revered and the country lived by the rules of Celtic society. We have an insight into how the people lived through the legends of the era. Celtic society was divided into clans, each with its own social structure, who lived in wattle and daub houses, within ring forts, farming the local lands. The Celts were warriors: they took pride in their weaponry, decorating their shields, helmets and battle horns. They fought on fast, agile chariots, pulled by two horses, with one person to steer and one to hurl spears at their opponents. They beheaded their victims and carried the heads of their past conquests on their belts or displayed them outside their homes.

Although the Celts were a tiered society, their respect for education and achievement meant that social mobility was possible. Rank was largely decided by property. Each person at any level would belong to one *fine* (their clan and social unit) and one *tuath* (their tribe and political unit).

At the top tier of society were the King, Bishop and High Poet, and next in rank were the nobles – also called kings but a lower level of king. After those were freemen – skilled traders, smiths, Druids and harpists – who owned property. Next in the hierarchy came the freemen who were without property and, finally, the non-free: labourers, workmen and lower-grade entertainers.

The King was not a judge or lawmaker in this society. Each king would represent their clan (*fine*) at regular assemblies called *oénach*. All members of the *tuath* would attend the *oénach*, which were used to declare new laws, conduct business deals and honour the dead (though only high-ranking members of society), as well as hold festivities, where there were games and horse racing. It is possible that these were funeral games, as they took place at tribal ceremonies, but it is equally probable that the community congregated at the old ritual ground.

DID YOU KNOW?

The Celts valued the arts, and poets held a high position in society.

DID YOU KNOW?

Druids held a role that merged the position of doctor, minister, political advisor, counsellor and judge. They were highly respected members of Celtic society.

DID YOU KNOW?

By the eighth century chariots were no longer used in battle but had become a sign of wealth.

MONASTERIES

By AD 550 Ireland was filled with monasteries and their missionaries were travelling across Europe, spreading the Christian message. Ireland became a place of refuge for persecuted Christians and those evading the barbarian invasions across the Roman Empire. By the seventh century, foreigners were coming to Ireland, particularly from England, to learn from the monasteries, which focused on community rather than reflection. The term 'monastery' (*monasterium*) referred to the buildings in the Roman Church but the Irish translation (*muintir*), which continues to be the word for family or community in modern Irish, referred to the people.

Monasteries were places of education but the schools for bards and lawyers still existed and these different places borrowed from each other's styles. The Irish system of learning by rote, rather than through writing, was introduced to the Church and in turn the history of Ireland began to be recorded by the literate Christians.

DID YOU KNOW?

Ireland is the only country where there were no martyrs as a result of Christian conversion.

DID YOU KNOW?

The 'fairy forts' that are seen across the country today are merely the earthen ramparts that were built around Celtic homes.

BREHON LAW

The people of Ireland were ruled by Brehon law from circa the fifth century. Travelling lawmakers, the Brehon (from the Old Irish word *brithem*, meaning 'adjudicator' or 'judge'), who were highly respected, learnt the law and were called upon to aid any cases. Brehon law was considered to come from nature and therefore it was of higher importance than the rules of Christianity. It existed until the seventeenth century and its official name was *feineachus*, but the new inhabitants of Ireland considered it barbaric. Nowadays, some people argue that Brehon law was more advanced and equal, though it's impossible to prove (and it would still be a matter of personal opinion).

The laws were largely practical and handed down orally through generations. Later, from the twelfth to the fourteenth century, manuscripts recorded the origins of the law as a form of precedent but also of storytelling. Historians believe that these manuscripts were most likely copied from earlier texts from the fifth century. Brehon law was a civil code made for and by the people, rather than the lawmakers who became its keepers. When Christians arrived in Ireland, they added to it, creating a system that tied the functional farming laws with religious morality. There were two strands of Brehon law: *cáin* law, which was national and could only be ruled by professional lawyers (who travelled the country, as mediators rather than judges), and *urradhus* law, which was local and could be decided by the clans. The adherence to the law was enforced locally and largely revolved around fines for wrongdoing. In extreme cases the perpetrator would be subject to blood atonement, though this was extremely rare; usually if someone injured another, they would be responsible for nursing their victim back to health.

Some excellent examples of Brehon law:
Any poet who overcharges for their poem can be stripped of half their rank in society.

If a spouse denies his pregnant wife any requested food because he is miserly or neglectful, he must pay a fine.

It is illegal to offer guests food that has been found with a dead mouse or weasel in it.

DID YOU KNOW?

Homosexuality was accepted by Celtic society, as long as both parties were not married. Under Brehon law it could be used as grounds for divorce, as could impotence, theft or telling details about your sex life.

VIKINGS

In 795 the Vikings attacked Iona Abbey, a monastery on the island of Iona, just off the western coast of Scotland. Over the following 40 years they continually attacked the Irish coast. Vikings, who hailed from across Scandinavia, arrived in longships with brightly coloured sails that were highly ornate. The warrior Vikings reached the Irish shores ready to plunder gold and burn wherever they went. Ireland in the ninth century was a land of separate clans and kingdoms, and as a result there was no collective effort to dispel these new colonisers. The Vikings learnt to aim for monasteries, as they held much wealth. They would sack the churches, taking the books and relics, though their interest was in the containers and covers that were made of precious stones and metals. The notion of the Vikings' ferocious appetites still survives today: according to the accounts left by the monks, who were their victims, they were fierce, ruthless and relentless; in reality, though, aside from their religious beliefs, they weren't very different from the Irish – craftsmen, sailors and farmers. Vikings were a mix of colonisers looking for land, traders looking for a market and pirates looking for a good haul. In 837 they began to attack as an army, in fleets, rather than lone vessels.

From 850 there are records of Irish alliances with Vikings against their local kings; working with the community, the Vikings became assimilated into Irish life. By the second half of the ninth century the power shifted away from the Vikings and back towards the Irish kings.

The Vikings began to build small towns in Ireland, both as trading centres and as ports. They created longphorts: enclosed fortresses – both temporary settlements for cold winter months and more permanent ones – of different size, some containing many buildings and some only a few. Regardless of size and permanence, each settlement was designed to best protect their most valued assets: their ships. One of the larger Viking longphorts was at the mouth of the river Liffey and evolved into Dublin city. Though they continued to raid towns and monasteries, their primary aim at this time was settlement, as is proven by the many bronze scales used to weigh the coins (whose value used to be determined by the weight of the gold or silver) that have been found by archaeologists, showing that there was a strong presence of traders.

When the Vikings began trading with the Irish, who had previously used a bartering system, they introduced a new age in Irish history: Ireland had entered into the world of commerce at last (we were pretty late to this game, which may act as some excuse for our subsequent troubled history with economics).

DID YOU KNOW?

More Irish metalwork, particularly silver and enamelled reliquaries (caskets for holy relics), has been found across Scandinavia than Ireland.

ART AND LEARNING

The ninth century also saw many new advances in art and scholarship in Ireland. Wooden huts began to be replaced by stone buildings, including the introduction of round towers, presumably showing the influence of returning missionaries and their descriptions of the belfries in Italy or the minarets of Eastern Europe and North Africa. In Ireland these towers, initially built to call the faithful to prayer, served another purpose after the Vikings began to invade, as the bell signified a warning and the building became a safe haven. Many of the round towers have doors that are out of reach of the ground so the monks, with their precious belongings, could climb up a ladder and then haul it into the tower, thus stopping the Vikings from entering. The survival of round towers showed that this tactic worked in many areas, though the building also functioned as a chimney and could be quickly destroyed by fire.

Stone sculpture began to develop at this time, and many ornate Celtic crosses, also known as high crosses, can be found throughout Ireland. Kells is famous for its five high crosses which are very ornate with Celtic knots and detailed patterns, as well as carvings of biblical stories such as Adam and Eve, Cain and Abel, and Daniel and the lions. The high crosses throughout Ireland show the skill and artistry of their sculptors, though they vary in the level of damage and decay.

RETURN OF THE IRISH KINGS

The Irish were still living in their divided kingdoms, overruled by a state system, and with the Norse in their towns. Their lives were relatively peaceful, for the era. This changed in 964 when a small and relatively unknown king, Mathgamain, captured Cashel from the Eóganachta. He went on to attack and defeat the Norse in Limerick. He died in battle in 976 but his brother Brian Boru continued his work, bringing all of Munster under his control.

BRIAN BORU'S QUEST FOR POWER

Brian Boru immediately set out to further his title, constantly attacking Máel Sechnaill, High King of Ireland since 980. After years of battles Máel submitted to Brian in 1002, making the latter High King of Ireland and self-titled 'Emperor of Ireland'. Brian quickly set to work, ensuring that he had control of the rest of the island. He marched north, taking hostages as a proof of strength, and then returned there in 1005, again attacking but also stopping in Armagh at the church established by St Patrick, now the Church of Ireland Cathedral, where he paid homage to the bishop. He gave 20 ounces of gold and was blessed, and his sovereignty was acknowledged and celebrated. This move would have ensured that any other warring bishops or bishop-kings would be slow to attack, as Brian was the High King in the eyes of the Church. Brian ruled for 12 years and in this time he made many good governing decisions, such as building or renovating bridges and roads, thus ensuring that the throughways for soldiers, messengers and ordinary citizens were accessible. He also rehabilitated monasteries, enabling better religious practices and learning. Throughout his time as High King, he was constantly fighting off opponents.

DID YOU KNOW?

Brian Boru was the last undisputed High King of Ireland.

THE IRISH TAKE DUBLIN

In 980, the Norse King Amlaíb Cuarán was defeated in Dublin by the Gaelic Irish of Meath, led by Máel Sechnaill mac Domnaill (from the Uí Néill clan), at the battle of Tara. This resulted in the Irish having control of Dublin, for the first time in its history. Máel Sechnaill besieged the city and gained power, looting and taking hostages. This marked the end of Viking rule in Ireland. The Norse remained part of Irish society, but didn't identify as Irish: although they held Norse beliefs and customs, they were no longer a united front, identified exclusively by their ethnicity.

Gormflaith was born in c.960. Her father, Murchadh mac Finn, was the king of Leinster. When Gormflaith was very young, she was married to Olaf Cuarán, the Norse king of Dublin and York, 42 years her senior. In 980 Gormflaith aided her husband's enemy, Máel Sechnaill mac Domnaill, king of Meath, to gain the throne as High King of Ireland by gathering the forces of her allies in Dublin and those of her brother, Mael Mórdha mac Murchada, King of Leinster. Olaf defected to Scotland. In 994 Máel Sechnaill and Gormflaith were then married, and her son Sitric Silkbeard was crowned king of Dublin. Brian Boru was gaining more power and attacked Máel Sechnaill. Gormflaith, seeing a star on the rise (or for who knows what reason), combined forces with her son Sitric – and, once again, with her brother Mael Mordha – and fought with Brian Boru against Máel Sechnaill in 999. Brian Boru became High King of Ireland and married Gormflaith. Their marriage was brief, though they had one son, Donnchad. When Brian divorced Gormflaith, Sitric and Mael Mordha attacked him, so he joined forces with Gormflaith's second husband, Máel Sechnaill. The result of this was the Battle of Clontarf, after which Gormflaith moved to a convent at Kincora, Munster, where she died in 1042.

BATTLE OF CLONTARF

In the years preceding the Battle of Clontarf the amount of skirmishes, raids and full-scale campaigns meant that a large conflict to settle the ruler of Ireland was seen as inevitable. Máel Sechnaill, who was the king of Meath – a seat always linked to the High King of Ireland – and Boru began an incessant round of skirmishes as they fought for the high kingship. In 997 they met and split Ireland in two, Maél taking the north and Boru the south. They each gave up hostages and declared peace. They joined forces in the battle of Glen Máma and defeated their rivals but after this Boru once again started to attack Máel Sechnaill. In 1000 Boru marched on Meath, attempting to win the seat of Tara with armies from Munster, Osraige, Leinster and Dublin. Máel Sechnaill defeated the Leinster and Dublin soldiers, and Boru was forced to retreat.

In 1002 he marched again, this time to Athlone, and took hostages from Connacht and Meath, ruining Máel Sechnaill's wealth and name. Cenél nEóghain, Cenél Conaill and Ulaid of the north soon acquiesced to Brian Boru when he marched through in 1011 – Boru was High King. The Norse king of Dublin, Sigtrygg, attempted to attack Meath, and later Cork, by sea. He travelled to Orkney, the Isle of Man, Denmark and Iceland, offering the kingship of Ireland if they defeated Brian, who united the Irish kings against a foreign invasion and attacked Dublin. There are varying accounts of the groups that fought with Brian, though all records agree that the Meath men deserted or changed sides. We know that his army went north of the Liffey and attacked as far as Howth, though apparently Brian did not go with them, instead choosing to stay behind to pray. Some records say he was too devout to fight on Good Friday. The Vikings halved their force, with one set joining Brian's men at Clontarf, leading the assault, and the others staying to protect Dublin. There were 16,000 Vikings fighting on the field that day, on both sides of the battle. Records say that 10,000 men were killed at the Battle of Clontarf. The day was given to Brian, though he had been killed in his tent by Bródir, a Danish warrior, who also died in battle.

END OF THE VIKING REIGN

The taking of Dublin at the Battle of Clontarf is usually considered the end of the Viking wars in Ireland, though in reality their reign had ended years before. By and large the Vikings had become Christian. Their crafts were influenced by Irish styles and skills, while in turn Irish craftsmen had equally been influenced by the Norsemen. Dublin had started minting the first Irish coins and was no longer dependent on Norse currency. Though the Viking age of power was over, their influence can still be seen in Ireland today, in place names and family names, as well as markets, towns and ports.

HISTORY (ELEVENTH-NINETEENTH CENTURY)

ELEVENTH CENTURY

The eleventh century was relatively uneventful in terms of battles, though skirmishes were frequent. Throughout this century, Ireland experienced something of a renaissance. The developments of the eleventh century led to the achievements of the twelfth century.

CROSS OF CONG

The cross of Cong, one of the finest examples of metalwork of the era, was a processional cross used to guide the clergy up the aisle. The cross was made in Roscommon, for Tairrdelbach Ua Conchobair, king of Connacht. Highly influenced by the

Scandinavian style, it is made of oak and covered in several different metals and minerals, including gold, silver, bronze, copper, brass, niello (a black alloy), enamel and glass. The shape of the cross is Romanesque, and it has Scandinavian-style strapwork and Hiberno-Saxon engraving. It was heavily bejewelled, though some of the beads and gems have been lost over time. Originally, it is said to have contained a 'piece of the true cross' sent from Rome in 1123. This was placed in a crystal and would have been visible to the congregation. The cross is on permanent display at the National Museum of Ireland – Archaeology, in Dublin.

MANUSCRIPTS

Artists began to mix old systems with new skills, and this can be seen particularly in manuscripts. Traditional Irish tales were recorded, as well as biblical stories and new poems that were being created. One example is *Fis Adamnán*, or *The Vision of Adamnán*, which was begun in the late tenth century and completed in the eleventh. It is one of the earliest examples of stories based on the trials of pilgrims. A precursor to Dante's *Divine Comedy*, as it had been widely translated, it may even have inspired him. It was also around this time that the monks started to record the genealogies of the Gaelic Irish which have offered vital information for historians ever since.

A huge amount of manuscripts were created during this century, a time which saw poets create new styles, reorganise their teaching methods and set up a grammatical rule system for the Irish language, the first of its kind in Western Europe.

CLOCHÁN

These monasteries – often referred to as 'beehive huts' – which had previously been made of wattle and daub, and then upgraded to wood, were finally built in stone. The stones were tightly packed in on top of each other without any mortar. These *Clochán* are primarily found in the southwest of the country and examples can still be seen today (and feature in the film *Star Wars: The Force Awakens*). They were essentially monks' cells, comprising an individual one-room round or rectangular hut with a dome roof.

CHURCH OF LAX RULES

From the fifth century until the death of Brian Boru in 1014, the Church in Ireland, though officially submissive to Rome, was essentially a self-governing institution. It took the initiative, beginning *c.*1000, under Brian's leadership, to rectify many of its failings. The Church's abuses of power carried on throughout the next two centuries, as churches and monasteries continued to be built, usually without seeking permission from Rome, leading to an abundance of monasteries that had no official connection to the Church. We can also see Ireland's religious influence in Germany with the *Schottenklöster* that Irish missionaries set up in Ratisbon, Würzburg, Erfurt and Mainz.

The Irish Church was very easy-going with the rules, and they had a mix of paganism and Christianity. It is possible that Brehon law had a hand in this, as the Irish people had two ruling bodies to adhere to, sometimes in conflict with each other. For example, most notably, the Church considered divorce to be sacrilegious but Brehon law allowed both parties to end a marriage, should they wish. Also, the Church in

Ireland allowed hereditary succession; Brehon lawyers and poets all learnt their skills, but they often hailed from families with generations of lawmakers or poets, and so it seemed right that priests could do the same. This meant that many bishops and Church officials had never taken holy orders but had merely used the title that their uncle or cousin had given them. The Church in Ireland at this time was monastic rather than diocesan and, as monasteries were insular institutions, no pastoral care was being offered, which also encouraged the lax attitude to the rules.

THE RIVALRY OF DERMOT MACMURROUGH AND TIERNAN O'ROURKE

Unlike what typically happens with invasions, the Norman invasion of Ireland was invited. Dermot MacMurrough (Diarmait Mac Murchada) was the king of Leinster and, like all of the kings of Ireland, had a long history of battles. In particular, Dermot and Tiernan O'Rourke had been constantly at war with each other for several decades. Things came to a head in 1152 when Dermot, to all appearances at the behest of Derbforgaill, the wife of O'Rourke, kidnapped her, mortifying his opponent. After this event O'Rourke joined forces with Ruaidri Ua Conchobair, the High King of Ireland, and set upon destroying the king of Leinster. In 1166 O'Rourke marched on Leinster with the High King's permission and deposed Dermot from his seat. Dermot fled to Wales, then England and finally France in a bid to get help from Henry II of England. With nothing to lose, Henry wrote a letter giving permission to his soldiers to fight for Dermot.

THE NORMAN INVASION
AND STRONGBOW

The first and most valuable of the mercenaries to agree to fight for Dermot was Richard de Clare, Earl of Pembroke, most commonly known as Strongbow. Out of favour with Henry II for his support of King Stephen and the Empress Matilda, Richard de Clare had nothing to lose. He drove a hard bargain and ensured that he would inherit the title of king of Leinster, as well as receiving the hand of Dermot's eldest daughter in marriage, whereas his fellow Normans were offered other lands across Leinster.

Strongbow did not land with the first attack on Ireland, which took the form of a short siege of Wicklow town. Instead, Dermot and his Norman invaders marched north, retaking Leinster and then moving into other kingdoms. The Norman invaders had far superior arms and quickly defeated each of the Gaelic kings. In 1170 Strongbow sent Raymond le Gros to Ireland and he proved to be an excellent fighter, quickly taking Waterford city. Strongbow landed in Waterford and, as agreed, was married to Dermot's daughter Aoife Ní Diarmait (often called Aoife MacMurrough or Red Eva) shortly after the city was taken. Dermot died soon after this and, though his son Donal MacMurrough-Kavanagh claimed his right to Leinster through Brehon law, Strongbow trumped his argument through negotiations and his subsequent marriage to Aoife. Strongbow sent his uncle Hervey de Montmorency to discuss terms with Henry II (as the 'help' they'd offered Dermot was in the name of the king) and was returned his lands (confiscated for supporting King Stephen and Empress Matilda) in England, France and Wales, as well as the Kingdom of Leinster. In return he had to give the powerful fortresses he'd captured, such as Dublin and Waterford, to Henry II. At this point the south and east of Ireland were under British rule, as both the Norman and the Gaelic lords accepted Henry II as king.

The Normans didn't have a systematic approach to ruling Ireland: Henry II offered the same lands to Gaelic tribes and Norman soldiers, and was too busy fighting the Continental wars to pay attention to what was happening on the small island west of Britain. The two sides unofficially divided up the country: with their superior weaponry, the Normans took the plains, coasts and riverways, and the Irish ruled the hills, bogs and woods.

DID YOU KNOW?

The Normans introduced the feudal system to Ireland, where the eldest son inherited the land and titles of his father. Prior to this, under Brehon law, land belonged to the *tuath* and kings would be elected into power rather than bequeathed the kingship.

DID YOU KNOW?

Strongbow was a posthumous nickname after both his weapon of choice and an inherited nickname from his father, but it was never used within his lifetime – his nickname then was Count Striguil because of the battle he won at Striguil.

FAMOUS FIGURES
AOIFE MACMURROUGH (c.1145-1188)

Aoife MacMurrough, as she is most commonly called – though her Gaelic name would have been Aoife Ní Diarmait and her official title after marriage was the Countess of Pembroke – was a force to be reckoned with. Though women were subservient, under Brehon law both parties had to agree to be married, so it is presumed that Aoife agreed to her father's plan for her nuptials. There is a presumption that Aoife and Strongbow must have had a personal agreement for his ruling of the land (though there is no written proof), as under Brehon law, Aoife had an interest in her father's land, though not ownership.

According to Anglo-Norman law, Strongbow had a right to Leinster through Aoife. Regardless of his wife's connection, according to Brehon law, land could be won, though not only Strongbow fought for Leinster. Aoife is known to have led men in battle, fighting for her right to Leinster, which earned her the name Red Eva.

DID YOU KNOW?

All of the wives of Henry VIII, except Anne of Cleves, were descendants of Strongbow and Aoife.

NORMAN SETTLEMENT

As the Normans ruled over their lands, they created lots of walled settlements and built castles. Under their influence commerce increased and agriculture was streamlined. They introduced a new currency, a concept that had never really taken off in Ireland prior to this time, as most people had continued to barter. Though the eastern part of the country was primarily under Norman control, outside of this region the Normans became assimilated into Irish society, adopting its customs as well as language. In 1297 counties were introduced in Ireland, using the same system of naming and granting lands that the Normans used in Scotland, Wales and England.

As the Normans were primarily town-based and loyal to their king, new laws were introduced in this period to give extra rights to townspeople. The Normans created a Parliament of Ireland in 1297. However, as time passed, Gaelic power reasserted itself. The lack of leadership from Henry III and his successor Edward I, who never visited Ireland and had more pressing matters with English and Welsh rebellions, as well as Crusades to the Holy Land, enabled the Irish to regain territory. The Normans began to support internal divisions within Gaelic society and fighting with Irish lords (no longer referred to as chieftains, as they had submitted to the king of England) – sometimes requesting support and other times offering it. In 1315 Edward Bruce invaded Ireland. Though he was defeated, his attack on the Norman settlements allowed the Gaelic lords to regain control of many of their lands. As the Wars of the Roses took hold, the English Crown was too distracted to become involved in the activities of the Irish Parliament.

TUDOR CONQUEST

In the sixteenth century the English Crown focused more on its neighbour once again. It began when the Earl of Kildare, known as Silken Thomas, rose up against the Crown. He had been running the country in the name of Henry VIII when, in 1534, he decided to take control. After quashing the rebellion, Henry VIII had himself declared king of Ireland by the Irish rather than the English Parliament. Each of the lords, both Norman and Gaelic, had to assert their loyalty to the Crown of England and in turn were granted their own lands back. In reality, the name of the leader of the country made very little difference to the Irish lords or the Irish people and they continued to live as they had before. Issues arose upon the death of Henry VIII, when successive Lord Deputies of Ireland discovered how little control the Crown had over the country. As they tried to assert power, the Irish began to rebel, with several revolts taking place between the 1550s and 1600s.

The English struggled to understand Irish law, which they didn't recognise, and though the Irish had technically been under British rule for centuries, the reality of being forced to live under another system created a huge amount of discontent. Under the governments of each of Henry VIII's successors, different tactics were attempted to quash the Irish rebellions. They tried to maintain power by using force, with the imposition of martial law, though pacification came with tax breaks and eventually plantations, whereby English and Scottish Protestants, loyal to the Crown, were granted confiscated lands. Aside from these issues, there was a further dilemma for the Crown when Pope Pius V declared Elizabeth I a heretic. This distanced her and her government from the Catholic majority in Ireland. The country became divided between the Irish, the Old English (of Norman extraction) and the English. The Old English became fervently Catholic and fought against the English lords, who were being granted lands.

NINE YEARS' WAR

The Nine Years' War was the largest of the rebellions of its time and was fought from 1594 to 1603. Hugh O'Neill, one of the most powerful Ulster chieftains ruling Tír Eoghain, teamed up with Hugh Roe O'Donnell, who ruled Tír Chonaill, in opposition to Queen Elizabeth. Prior to this, many of the rebellions sought to regain personal power but Hugh O'Neill was determined to end British rule in Ireland. England was at the end of a long period of struggles and found it difficult to get numbers for its armies, needing to resort to conscription to force people to go to war. The troops were young, untrained and unwilling (hundreds absconded before reaching Ireland and as many again once they arrived there). O'Neill was a powerful adversary and a wonderful tactician, luring the British soldiers into bogs and ambushing them as they marched, exhausted, through the country.

Seeing the success of the Ulster rebellion, other parts of Ireland started to rise up against the Crown. Munster began to attack and the English settlers returned to England. Elizabeth sent a new group of loyal seasoned commanders to Ireland who, at first, began talks but these proved unsuccessful. In 1601 George Carew regained control of Munster and in the same year the Spanish arrived. England had been at war with Spain and O'Neill made a deal with the Spanish king, Philip III, who sent troops, though they were quickly defeated. The English marched into Ulster and O'Donnell went to Spain to plead for more help but he died while there, supposedly poisoned by an English secret agent. O'Neill destroyed his own settlement at Dungannon and retreated to the woods.

The English Army under Lord Mountjoy began a scorched earth policy in Northern Ireland which caused a famine. As the Irish lords began to surrender, Hugh O'Neill held out for longer. He eventually signed the Treaty of Mellifont and received good terms, largely because Elizabeth I had died six days before he capitulated. The treaty stipulated that the Irish lords could no longer use their Irish titles, could no longer hold a private army and could not control their dependents. At this point the English coffers were empty (as no doubt were the Irish ones) and James I was eager to put an end to a war that had cost England over £2 million – a massive amount for the time.

DID YOU KNOW?

Shakespeare wrote *Richard II*, *Henry IV* (parts 1 and 2) and *Henry V* between 1596 and 1599. His comments on the Irish in these plays are a thinly veiled commentary on the Nine Years' War.

FLIGHT OF THE EARLS

In 1607, dissatisfied with their loss of power, O'Neill and Rory O'Donnell (the brother of Hugh Roe) left Ireland in the hope of finding military backers to support another uprising. They travelled first to France and then to the Spanish Netherlands, finally settling in Italy. O'Donnell died from a fever shortly after, in 1608, and in 1614 King James reclaimed their titles. O'Neill lived in Rome, having been granted a papal pension. He died in 1616, also from a fever, and was interred next to O'Donnell in the church of San Pietro in Montorio. After their deaths, despite their titles being forfeit, O'Donnell and O'Neill's sons continued to use them, leading to a political and legal quagmire, as Catholics both within Ireland and on the Continent continued to recognise the two earls' descendants, though there were formally no earldoms.

THE 1641 REBELLION

Despite the rise in plantations and influx of Scottish and English Protestants, Ireland was still predominantly Catholic. In 1605 the Gunpowder Plot, a failed English Catholic plot to blow up the Houses of Parliament, incited the Crown to create laws curtailing the rights of Catholics, and particularly their access to wealth and power. This meant that, for the first time, the English Protestants had a majority in the Irish Parliament. After enduring several years of diminished influence, several Catholic lords sought an audience with King James and, later, King Charles I. They agreed that, in return for paying more taxes, he would grant them religious tolerance and land security. In 1630 the Irish Catholic lords paid more taxes (although Charles delayed the fulfilment of his part of the deal until 1641). In 1638 the Scottish rose up against Charles I and, after failing for two years to quash the rebellion, the king recruited an army of Catholics from Ireland, offering in return full rights to own lands and to practise their religion.

Phelim O'Neill took control of some northern towns and read out a proclamation, in the name of Charles I, which supported him defending Ireland against Protestants and asked for all of Ireland to support him. The proclamation was a forgery but, unaware of this, many of the Catholic lords of Ireland supported him.

The government sent mercenaries to the south of Ireland to destroy the rebellion. They were ruthless and indiscriminate in whom they attacked, leading to more support for the rebellion. In the north of the country the Catholic peasantry began to attack Protestant settlers and despite O'Neill's attempts to stop this, he was unable to control the Catholics. It wasn't long before this led to devastating massacres which spread throughout Ireland, and soon Catholics in Munster were also attacking their Protestant neighbours. The scale of the atrocities is unknown – numbers between 12,000 and 200,000 have been put forward – but the effect, particularly in Ulster, was the creation of a rift that continues to this day.

EFFECTS OF THE ENGLISH CIVIL WAR IN IRELAND

In 1642 Charles I sent a large army to quell the rebels. Scotland also sent troops to Ulster to help. However, the English Civil War broke out and Parliament withdrew the troops from Ireland to fight on home soil. The Irish established the Irish Catholic Confederation and swore allegiance to Charles I. In 1649, once the English republicans had gained control of England, they sent Oliver Cromwell and his army over to Ireland. Cromwell was ruthless and brutal, and he installed harsher laws on Catholicism than had previously existed. Catholics were massacred by Cromwell's forces and over 300,000 of them either died or were deported to work as indentured labourers. By 1653 power in Ireland was back in the hands of the Protestant settlers and the English authorities.

The re-establishment of the monarchy in England in 1660 meant that the control Cromwell had on Ireland dissipated. The new lords expected King Charles II to uphold the titles given by Cromwell, and the Catholic lords hoped to have their lands reinstated. Charles attempted to create a compromise, under which 20 per cent of Ireland went back to Catholic lordship.

DID YOU KNOW?

After leaving Ireland in 1650, Cromwell was sent to Scotland because the Scots had proclaimed Charles II as king.

JAMES II AND THE GLORIOUS REVOLUTION

In 1685 James II, the Catholic son of Charles II, succeeded to the throne. Protestant nobles were worried about a Catholic on the throne and soon rebelled, offering the throne to James's son-in-law, William of Orange, and his daughter Mary. James II had a large army but when William and Mary landed, he did not attack (no one is entirely sure why, but the official line is that he 'lost confidence'). Upon being caught, he was imprisoned but escaped and fled to France. Parliament (after the recent republic) did not want to depose the king but declared that, by fleeing, James II had effectively abdicated. A law was created to make it illegal for any monarch of England to marry a Catholic, which was only repealed in 2011. In 1689, James II went to Ireland to raise an army to fight against William of Orange, and the following year the Battle of the Boyne took place in County Meath. William's army crushed James's army and he fled back to France. This battle solidified the control of the Protestant elite in Ireland. William of Orange offered Irish lords their land in return for allegiance, a deal which some of them – though few – accepted.

DID YOU KNOW?

Catholics maintained allegiance to James II and continued to consider his son the true king of England until his death in 1766.

REPEAL OF THE PENAL LAWS

After the end of the War of the Spanish Succession in 1714, and simply thanks to the passage of time, the Penal Laws that had discriminated against Catholic lords began to be retracted, as they proved to be no threat. Inspired by the American Revolution, the Irish began to fight for emancipation. England had sent most of its troops to America and called on Ireland to supply troops for protection against a French invasion, as France supported the Americans. Ireland used this as a bartering tool to gain more rights and aim for Home Rule. The Irish Volunteers were established; they protected Ireland from invasion and kept order. These men argued for Catholic emancipation and some of the Penal Laws were repealed. These changes allowed Catholics to work in public office, intermarry with Protestants, vote and benefit from other freedoms. Each repeal had to be fought for and the whole process took nearly 100 years. The majority of reformers were peaceful and achieved change by fighting through the courts and Parliament. However, there were those who were tired of waiting and this led to the 1798 Irish Rebellion.

THE 1798 REBELLION

Inspired by the revolutions of France and America, Theobald Wolfe Tone started a group called the Society of United Irishmen. This group lobbied for the rights of all Irish people and to break ties with England. When they failed to gain traction by peaceful means, the Society planned an insurrection across Ireland. The Dublin uprising failed but the rest of the country rebelled. Across Ireland each of the revolts was quickly quashed, except for the one in Wexford. In support of Wexford, Co. Antrim rose up and when they were defeated, Co. Down rebelled. This was also quickly suppressed by the English. Those in Wexford were still in battle, though they had left the towns and absconded to the hills. The British sent 20,000 troops to attack Vinegar Hill and the rebels died in their hundreds. Wolfe Tone was caught on a boat headed for France and was tried for treason, in Dublin, and executed. The 1798 Rebellion changed the course of Irish history: from then on the Irish continually fought for an Irish republic.

DID YOU KNOW?

The Wexford Rebellion was led by a priest, Father John Murphy.

ACT OF UNION

The Act of Union 1800 sought to dissolve the 1782 constitution that gave independence to the Irish Parliament, thus making

Ireland, once again, answerable to Westminster. After recently losing America, and as the war with France continued, Prime Minister William Pitt focused on maintaining control over Ireland. The Act was passed, largely because of the promise of Catholic emancipation. Also, the rebellion was viewed as a reaction to loyalist brutality and London wanted to ensure that, with Catholics being able to hold office, further bloodshed could be avoided, while Britain continued to maintain control over Ireland. The Irish lords fought the Act of Union, fearing the loss of their autonomy over Irish law but the people wanted the Act to pass, hoping this would speed along the change in Catholic rights. The Irish Anglican parliamentarians stalling the Act of Union finally conceded (most receiving peerages and honours in compensation) and it was passed, in both England and Ireland.

DID YOU KNOW?

The flag of the United Kingdom was created after the Act of Union 1800 was passed. Commonly called the 'Union Jack', and still in use today, it combines the flags for St George, St Andrew and St Patrick.

ROBERT EMMET AND THE REBELLION OF 1803

Very little changed after the Act of Union. Robert Emmet, an Irish Anglican Member of Parliament, sympathised with Irish Catholics' lack of representation at Parliament and worked with the United Irish Society, trying to reorganise them after their defeat in the 1798 Rebellion. In 1799 the British authorities called for his arrest but he escaped to Europe in hope of finding support for his cause. This was unsuccessful, as Europe was in the midst of the Napoleonic Wars. He returned to Ireland and began to plan for a rebellion in 1803. He manufactured explosives and gathered weapons but one of the properties where he was making and storing the ammunition exploded. Emmet was forced to move his rebellion forward to make sure they still had the element of surprise. Worried about their lack of preparation and with fewer firearms than expected, many of the rebels withdrew. On 23 July 1803 the rebels released 10,000 copies of their proclamation in the name of the 'provisional government'. The rebellion failed and after witnessing a man being brutally killed, Emmet attempted to call off the insurgents, but it was too late. They committed random acts of violence, most notably stabbing people to death with pikes, before being quashed by the British. Emmet was tried for treason and sentenced to the death penalty. His speech from the dock went down in history and was often quoted by Irish nationalists.

The final words of Emmet's speech

Let no man write my epitaph; for as no man who knows my motives dare now vindicate them, let not prejudice or ignorance asperse them. Let them and me rest in obscurity and peace, and my name remain uninscribed, until other times and other men can do justice to my character. When my country takes her place among the nations of the earth, then, and not till then, let my epitaph be written. I have done.

DID YOU KNOW?

Anne Devlin was Robert Emmet's housekeeper. When asked to inform on him, she refused bribes and so was sent to prison and tortured. Her entire family were imprisoned and the conditions led to her nine-year-old brother's death. Anne was in prison for several years, long after Emmet had been hanged, drawn and quartered. She never gave any information to her interrogators.

DANIEL O'CONNELL AND CATHOLIC EMANCIPATION

Daniel O'Connell was an Irish political leader who campaigned for Catholic emancipation and a repeal of the Act of Union. He was a qualified barrister but, as a Catholic, he was not able to take any high office; after studying in France he was admitted to Lincoln's Inn, London, and then to King's Inns, Dublin. O'Connell was passionate about Irish heritage and freedom but he did not support the 1798 Rebellion. He believed that the only way to achieve equality was through discussion and treaty. He became a very successful barrister and in 1813 established the Catholic Board, which campaigned for Catholics to become Members of Parliament. In 1823 he set up the Catholic Association, which fought for several rights for Catholics and whose membership fees were purposely kept very low, in order to attract the Irish peasantry. The huge uptake made the Association a financial success, funding many pro-emancipation campaigns. O'Connell used this group to encourage local people to vote for pro-emancipation candidates rather than their landlord or local lord, as they usually did. The move succeeded but landlords began to evict tenants in retribution for their perceived disloyalty.

In 1828 O'Connell stood for a seat in Parliament for County Clare and won by a landslide, though he was unable to take his seat as he was a devout Catholic and the Oath of Supremacy required acknowledging the British monarch as God's representative on Earth. Fearing a backlash from the Irish people for not allowing him to take his seat, the Duke of Wellington and Robert Peel advised George IV to repeal the law barring other religions from sitting in Parliament. In 1829 the Roman Catholic Relief Act was signed into law. Although this law permitted Catholics to vote and become Members of Parliament, the property qualification for voters was increased to five times the previous value, ensuring that most Catholics remained ineligible to vote. The Act was nevertheless considered a huge step forward and O'Connell was nicknamed 'the Liberator', in commemoration of his achievements.

DID YOU KNOW?

O'Connell was challenged to a duel by John D'Esterre and won. He abhorred that he had taken another person's life and offered to share his income with D'Esterre's widow, who refused, though she did accept an allowance for her daughter. O'Connell paid this allowance for over 30 years, until his death.

O'Connell then set his sights on overturning the Act of Union 1800. Though he had support in England for the emancipation of Catholics, very few members of the House of Lords were interested in Ireland having its own parliament. O'Connell founded the Repeal Association in 1830 and held gatherings, nicknamed 'monster meetings', throughout the country. Thousands of people would assemble to hear O'Connell speak and to show the British Parliament the extent of the public's support for Home Rule for Ireland. Prime Minister Peel then banned a monster meeting that was set for 8 October 1843 and sent in armed cavalry. O'Connell called off the meeting, fearing it would descend into violence. Regardless of this, he was arrested and sentenced to a year in prison, though he was released after three months. The Repeal Association then began to split, with many people joining the Young Irelanders, who believed that violence was necessary to achieve a free Ireland. O'Connell died on a pilgrimage in Italy, having been severely weakened by his time in prison.

DID YOU KNOW?

Carrying green flags or banners was against the law so people would carry green boughs to show their support for Irish Home Rule.

HISTORY (NINETEENTH-TWENTIETH CENTURY)

THE GREAT FAMINE

The Great Famine was a natural disaster that escalated dramatically due to British policy. This in turn led to an uprising that was supported by a large section of the Irish population who had become embittered towards English rule. The anti-Catholic Penal Laws dictated that Catholics had to divide their land between all of their sons, thus reducing the size of Catholic-owned holdings with each generation. As Protestants were not bound by the Penal Laws, their ownership of the land of Ireland increased from 10 per cent in 1600 to 95 per cent in 1778, leaving Catholics to live in abject poverty on very small patches of land.

Most people were charged high rents to live on these small plots and this led to their dependence on crops that provided ample sustenance but needed little space to thrive. By the 1800s, the potato had become the staple food in the poorest regions. More than three million Irish peasants subsisted solely on this vegetable, which is rich in protein, carbohydrates, minerals and vitamins such as riboflavin, niacin and vitamin C. It is possible to stay healthy on a diet of potatoes alone. Peasants often drank a little buttermilk with their meal and sometimes used salt, cabbage and fish as seasoning.

DID YOU KNOW?

Irish peasants were actually healthier than peasants in England or Europe where bread, far less nutritious, was the staple food.

In the 1840s a potato blight swept across parts of the country and began to destroy the crops. The plant above the soil would look unchanged but below the ground the potatoes had turned to rotten black mulch. The Famine began in 1845, when about half of the potato crop was destroyed by blight. In the first year of the Famine, deaths from starvation were kept down due to the imports of Indian corn and the survival of about half of the original potato crop. Poor Irish people survived those initial months by selling off their livestock and possessions, borrowing from moneylenders and falling behind on their rents.

The potato crop in Ireland had never failed for two consecutive years but, catastrophically, weather conditions in the summer of 1846 were ideally suited to the spread of potato blight, which resulted in another crop disaster – and this time there were no reserves left for people to survive on.

Throughout the Famine years, large quantities of native-grown wheat, barley and oats were shipped to England, even though the

Irish people were dying of starvation. Irish farmers, desperate for cash, routinely sold the grain to the British in order to pay the rent on their farms and avoid eviction.

Between 1845 and 1849 over one million people died and another million emigrated. The British government took the economic decision not to interfere, afraid that Ireland might become dependent on handouts. Sir Charles Trevelyan, assistant secretary to the Treasury and the man in charge of relief schemes, considered the Famine a judgement from God and a practical way to deal with the surplus population of Ireland. Theories abound, claiming that the refusal to help was a systematic genocide aimed at repressing possible future rebellions – labelling the Irish Famine a genocide is still divisive, though.

Many charities and religious institutions began to hand out food but they simply didn't have the means to deal with this epidemic. Added to this, the Anglican Church insisted that those who received from their soup kitchens had to convert to their religion and, in order to ensure that people did not lie, they would serve meat on a Friday, as Catholics could not eat it. Soon cholera, dysentery and typhoid began to spread. Emigration continued in big numbers until 1855. The ships were known as 'coffin ships' because so many people died on the long journeys to the New World.

DID YOU KNOW?

To this day, the population of Ireland has not recovered to its pre-famine level. The 1841 census recorded 8.2 million people in Ireland, though 8.5 million is considered more accurate. In the 2016 census Ireland's population had grown by 3.7 per cent since the 2011 census to just under 4.8 million.

DID YOU KNOW?

In 1858 a new group established itself to fight for independence. The Irish Republican Brotherhood (IRB) – also known as the Fenians – was a secret society, as its initial aim was to rise up in rebellion against the English. A sister organisation, called Clan na Gael, was organised in New York amongst the Irish émigrés. This movement had very little support and their attempt to stage a rising in 1867 failed miserably.

LAND WAR

After the Famine, tenant farmers began to campaign for better rights. This 'Land War' was framed within a nationalist perspective. The tenant farmers argued that the land they worked on had been taken, unjustly, from their ancestors. The Irish National Land League was founded in Castlebar, Co. Mayo, in 1879 and Charles Stewart Parnell was elected as its president. The Land League wanted the 'three Fs – Fair rent, Free sale and Fixity of tenure'. Many of the prominent members of the movement were also members of the IRB.

The Land War was a campaign (rather than a war in the more literal sense of the word) to raise awareness for the national cause. The Irish began to boycott unpopular landlords, refusing to pay rents, refusing to work and even refusing to serve them in local shops, which proved very effective. When landlords tried to evict tenants, things became violent. Prime Minister Benjamin Disraeli introduced martial law in Ireland and imprisoned the leaders of the Land League, in an attempt to contain the violence. By the 1880s successive acts gave the farmers more rights to own land and rural affairs were run on a local level. However, this did not end the political unrest as the British Government had hoped.

DID YOU KNOW?

The verb 'boycott' originates from Captain Charles Cunningham Boycott, a land agent for Lord Erne, a Mayo landowner. When Boycott raised the rents on the local farmers, the community ostracised him completely.

FAMOUS FIGURES
CHARLES STEWART PARNELL (1846-1891)

Charles Stewart Parnell was an Irish nationalist politician and one of the leaders of the Land League and Home Rule League. He was an extremely powerful politician and is generally considered responsible for the eventual passage of the Home Rule for Ireland Bill. Elected to Parliament in 1875 as a member of the Home Rule League, Parnell considered the reform of the land laws to be a first step towards righting injustice and gaining Home Rule for Ireland. In 1880 he supported the Liberal leader William Gladstone in the general election but when the latter fell short of his promises for land reform, Parnell joined the opposition. Parnell was an instigator in the boycott movement and in 1882 he once again had talks with Gladstone and offered his support for the first Irish Home Rule Bill. The Liberal Party was split. The Bill didn't pass and Gladstone's government fell. *The Times* printed a letter alleging that Parnell supported the Phoenix Park Murders (the killing of two British officials in Dublin that he had publicly condemned) but he managed to prove that it was a forgery and won the support of the English Liberals. His success was short-lived, though, as his longstanding affair with Kitty O'Shea was made public by her husband when he filed for divorce. Due to this scandal, Parnell's popularity plummeted. Without support from the Liberals and with his own party – the Irish Parliamentary Party – split in two (the Irish National League, or pro-Parnellites, on one side and the Irish National Federation, or anti-Parnellites, on the other), the Home Rule Bill failed. Parnell continued to fight but died soon after this, in 1891.

DID YOU KNOW?

By 1900 the Irish language was no longer widely used in Ireland. To drive support for the nationalist cause and to separate the Irish from the British, nationalists began a Gaelic revival. Different organisations were set up to promote Irish language, culture and sport. Though the cultural and sports organisations became popular, the Irish language remained in decline.

SEEDS OF REBELLION

After the general election of 1910 the Irish Parliamentary Party (now reunited) held the balance of power in the House of Commons where, in 1912, another Home Rule Bill was put forward and passed, though it was blocked by the House of Lords. In the two-year hiatus after the vote (before the Bill could be reintroduced) the Houses continued to discuss Irish Home Rule. In Ireland, both sides – the pro-Home Rule Irish Volunteers and the anti-Home Rule Ulster Volunteer Force – became active militants, drilling openly.

Ireland was an island of extremes of wealth. In answer to the abject poverty some people lived in, social reformers like James Larkin and James Connolly began a trade union movement. In Ulster, the Belfast Dockers went on strike for better pay and conditions, and in Dublin in 1913 more than 20,000 workers were fired for being members of a trade union, resulting in vicious riots that led to many injuries and three deaths. James Connolly created the Irish Citizen Army for strikers to defend themselves from the police. Despite their similar intentions, the trade unions were not united. In southern Ireland the socialist and labour movement tied in with Irish republicans, though most nationalists did not approve of the leftist social agenda. In Ulster the trade unions aligned themselves with British trade union organisations.

Irish Home Rule was finally passed in 1914, but deferred until the end of World War One. Ireland was further split between nationalists believing that fighting with the British would ensure that the Home Rule Bill would be enacted after the war and others convinced that this was the best time to attack and achieve a republic. Most Dubliners left the Irish Citizen Army when they became aware that Connolly sympathised with the IRB. The Ulster Volunteer Force in the north and the Irish Volunteers in the south pledged to fight for Britain. Over 100,000 men went to fight from the Irish Volunteers led by John Redmond and 12,000 remained in Ireland under the leadership of Eoin MacNeill, who wanted Ireland to remain neutral. MacNeill was a pacifist, but the IRB infiltrated the Irish Volunteers, gathering recruits.

By 1915 the Citizen Army were clamouring for a rising. The IRB were planning a rebellion and they didn't want Connolly to start something that might have the British on high alert. So the IRB convinced him to wait and take part in their revolution. Connolly joined six others – Tom Clarke, Sean MacDermott, Padraig Pearse, Eamonn Ceannt, Joseph Plunkett and Thomas MacDonagh – as a member of the IRB's Military Council. The plan was to hold a rising on Good Friday, 21 April 1916, with the aid of German weapons and troops, though both failed to materialise.

The Irish sent Sir Roger Casement to gather troops, after Germany offered the opportunity to recruit from their prisoners of war, hoping to split British forces and gain another attack route to Britain without the need to involve German soldiers. Casement and his anti-British sentiment offended the majority of Irish prisoners of war, who had survived unquestionable horrors and were loyal to the British Army and the soldiers still fighting – he managed to recruit only 56 men. The Germans also offered as support a ship that could shoot from Dublin Bay. The rebellion was postponed till Easter Sunday, 23 April, but the message failed to reach Germany on time so the ship arrived on 21 April and the Irish were unaware that it had landed.

EASTER RISING

The Easter Rising was not as much of a surprise as many people think. The British were aware of the plot, but decided that going on the offensive might incite a larger revolution. Eoin MacNeill learnt of the rebellion and countermanded the order, badly affecting the amount of people taking part. With reduced numbers, the rebellion went ahead on Easter Monday. It lasted for seven days and was largely unsupported by the Irish public. After the rising, the British shot the leaders, without public trial, by firing squad. This act of brutality, particularly in the cases of Connolly – who was tied to a chair as he was too ill to stand due to injuries sustained during the fighting – and Plunkett, who married his sweetheart and was shot immediately after, turned the tide of public opinion.

DID YOU KNOW?

During the rising, both sides put down their guns each day so the ducks in St Stephen's Green could be fed.

In 1918 Britain attempted to introduce compulsory conscription in Ireland. This was met by widespread opposition from nationalist political and religious leaders, and the Irish Party officially withdrew its MPs from Westminster. Resistance to conscription greatly increased the popularity and credibility of Sinn Féin, a new party made up of nationalists. Sinn Féin won a large majority of the Irish seats in the general election on a platform that included the boycott of Westminster in favour of an assembly in Ireland. Following the election, the successful Sinn Féin candidates formed a parliament in Dublin, the First Dáil, which declared Irish independence as a republic.

DID YOU KNOW?

Constance Markievicz (née Gore-Booth) was the first woman voted into the British Parliament, though she never took her seat. She sat in Dáil Éireann instead.

WAR OF INDEPENDENCE

On 21 January 1919, while the Dáil was meeting in Ireland, two police officers were killed by republican volunteers in Co. Tipperary. The British responded by putting the entire area under martial law – the Irish War of Independence had begun. The Irish used guerrilla tactics to fight the British forces, made up of the British Army and paramilitary police known as the Auxiliary Division or the Black and Tans. Both sides were brutal in their treatment of the other. Britain began to discuss Home Rule and, as the nationalists no longer attended Westminster, the agreement was made with the Ulster Unionists. This meant that Catholic views were not represented when Ireland was being divided, which later had significant ramifications, particularly with Catholic representation in Northern Ireland. Established in 1921, Northern Ireland did not include Donegal and Cavan, as these Ulster counties were largely Catholic.

Ulster was a powerhouse of linen and shipbuilding, and the British were interested in maintaining these ties. The Ulster Unionists, who were mostly Protestant and identified as British, welcomed Britain's economic strength. In July 1921 the Anglo-Irish Treaty was drawn up, establishing the Irish Free State, as well as the Irish Boundary Commission to discuss the details of the border within the island.

DID YOU KNOW?

In the 1920s 43 per cent of Irish-born people lived abroad. By comparison, in 2015, even after the mass emigration caused by the most recent economic recession, the proportion only reached 17 per cent.

In Northern Ireland the police force – the Royal Ulster Constabulary (RUC) – the B Specials (a military-reserve special constable force) and a new Parliament were set up. In 1932 the Parliament moved to Stormont in East Belfast, outside of the city centre, where it remains today. The Parliament showed a preference for the Protestant population, offering them better economic, housing and social support. In reality, the mentality of Catholics and Protestants hadn't changed in Northern Ireland since the establishment of the unionist militia, the Ulster Volunteer Force (UVF), and the nationalist militia, the Irish Volunteers. Both sides continued to fight, with small groups targeting each other, though the loyalists were in official uniform whereas the nationalists remained a paramilitary organisation.

When the Anglo-Irish Treaty was being signed in 1921, the split among politicians and the people of the new Irish Free State between pro-Treaty and anti-Treaty led to the Irish Civil War. The Treaty gave all but six counties in Ireland independence from England, though it kept Ireland's allegiance intact, rescinding the Republic that had been declared in 1916 and 1918. The pro-Treaty side commanded a majority in the Dáil and the Act was passed. The anti-Treaty side, led by Eamon de Valera, who had resigned as a minister with two others in protest, continued to fight as insurgents. This group occupied the Four Courts and were the ones blamed when a retired British general was shot dead in London (though they never accepted this). The British government insisted that the Irish government take action. The pro-Treaty faction became Ireland's National Army and in 1922 attacked the Four Courts, starting the Irish Civil War. The country was split between these two groups, and IRA groups were forced to take a side. The anti-Treaty side reverted to guerrilla war tactics, leading a campaign of assassinations and destruction of property, while the pro-Treaty side was supported and supplied by the British. The new Irish Government began a series of executions and with many losses, on both sides, civilians (the anti-Treaty group) were told to cease fire and return home, effectively ending the war, though neither side ever negotiated any terms of peace.

DID YOU KNOW?

In 1937 the Irish ratified the Irish Constitution, breaking all ties with Britain. This Constitution established the role of the Dáil (lower house), Seanad (upper house) and Uachtarán (President).

WORLD WAR TWO

The Republic of Ireland remained neutral, in theory, during World War Two, though the few soldiers who landed there (usually because of plane crashes) were treated differently. British soldiers were returned to England to continue fighting, whereas German soldiers were kept in Ireland. British forces were allowed to fly over Ireland, which remained dependent on British imports. Ireland also negotiated its security with Germany as a neutral country. On the other hand, Northern Ireland was heavily involved in World War Two and Belfast's shipping ports were targeted by the Germans. The same amount of recruits volunteered to fight for Britain from north and south of the border.

The IRA continued to be active in their fight to unify Ireland until 1948 when the country became a republic. The IRA then focused their attention on Northern Ireland, with the same aim.

Throughout the 1950s the Republic of Ireland was extremely poor and, again, the country experienced mass emigration. In the 1960s Seán Lemass, as Taoiseach (prime minister), steered the country towards free trade and brought in foreign investment to boost the economy. In 1973 both the Republic of Ireland and Britain joined the European Economic Community (EEC), which later became the European Union (EU). Ireland's economy grew with the EEC, though it was hard hit during a recession in the 1980s, which again led to mass emigration. As many of the young left, the country became very conservative, voting against abortion in 1983 and against divorce in 1986.

BLOODY SUNDAY AND THE TROUBLES

Northern Ireland remained in a state of unrest due to the tit-for-tat nature of the attacks between nationalists and unionists. After World War Two, health and social care were the focus of the new British government but the Catholic population in Northern Ireland were still living in a state of social deprivation, as the province was administered unequally by a sectarian government. In 1967, Catholics began to march, protesting against their living conditions. The Civil Rights Movement was peaceful but, in 1968, peaceful demonstrators were attacked by the police force (the RUC). Images of the attack were publicised across the world and there was international outrage at the RUC's actions.

In 1969 the Bogside area of Derry set up barricades to stop an Orange March from passing through their Catholic area. These barricades led to a full riot, and the British Army were called in to help restore order. The IRA retaliated with violent crimes against the police and army personnel. The army originally entered the country to protect the Catholics, but once they and their families began to be personally attacked, they fought with the same repressive tactics as the RUC. The British government introduced internment without trial, which allowed them to arrest and jail anyone they considered a possible threat. In 1972 the situation escalated when British soldiers shot 26 unarmed civilians, 13 of them fatally, during a peaceful march in Derry, Northern Ireland. This day was called 'Bloody Sunday': protestors were shot, beaten and run down by police vehicles. In retaliation, the IRA exploded around 20 car bombs in Belfast on a day that became known as 'Bloody Friday'.

STRIKES IN H BLOCK

The Troubles exacerbated a deep-seated resentment between the Catholic and Protestant communities. Many Protestants were victims of nationalist terrorist organisations, mainly the IRA, while many Catholics were the victims of loyalist paramilitary organisations such as the UVF and UDA. The sectarian nature of government administration, unfairly favouring Protestants, maintained a sense of deprivation and disadvantage within the Catholic community. The new law that enabled anyone to be imprisoned without trial targeted Catholics and created a large group of nationalists in the prisons, which became a recruitment ground for the IRA, whose members considered themselves political prisoners in a war of independence. As most had been interned without trial, they were considered to have 'special category' status but in 1976 the new British government wanted to eliminate this distinction so that all prisoners would be considered equal. Prisoners in H Block of Long Kesh prison in Maze, County Down – nicknamed 'The Maze' – began to protest against this change. The abolition of 'special category' status was equally unpopular with loyalists (five per cent of internees were loyalist) who didn't feel that ordinary criminals should be considered to be the same as terrorists.

In 1976, Kieran Nugent began a blanket protest, refusing to wear a prison uniform (he wore his blanket draped over his shoulders instead) because previously political prisoners were not required to wear prison uniforms, as they considered themselves revolutionaries rather than criminals. Others joined him. They were confined to their cells for 24 hours a day and no longer had the chance of early release. They then destroyed some of the furniture in their cells so everything was taken away except the Bible, a mattress and three blankets each (there were two people per cell).

In 1978, prisoners were no longer permitted a second towel to wash themselves. They were expected to stand naked in the washrooms so they protested by refusing to leave their cells. What began with prisoners no longer washing (no-wash protest) escalated when later they famously started to smear their cell walls with their faeces and pour their urine out of the windows in a dirty protest. Nugent and three other prisoners appealed to the European Commission on Human Rights about their inhumane treatment but the court rejected the case, as the treatment was self-inflicted, though they stated that the British government was being 'inflexible'. When the Archbishop of Armagh visited the prison in 1978, he publicised the treatment of the men inside: how they were beaten by guards and subjected to cruel treatment, such as intimate searches and having their mattresses taken away and urine being swept into their cells. The prison authorities' response to the report was that the prisoners had inflicted this upon themselves.

HUNGER STRIKES

By 1980 nearly half the republican prisoners were involved in the dirty protest, which was strategically called off a year later to focus public attention on a more extreme form of protest: hunger strikes. There were two hunger strikes at the Maze: the first one began in 1980 and ended when the prisoners wrongly believed that their demands had been met. The second strike, organised by Bobby Sands (leader of the Provisional IRA prisoners), began on 1 March 1981. Sands ensured that the strike was staggered, so a new striker would join each week, thus sustaining pressure on the government. Four days into the strike, the MP for Fermanagh and South Tyrone died suddenly. Sinn Féin nominated Sands for the vacant seat and he was elected on 9 April, despite being incarcerated in the Maze and becoming increasingly ill from starvation. Margaret Thatcher's government refused to converse with the hunger strikers and 66 days after he began his strike, Bobby Sands died. Three more strikers died soon after but the British government refused to open talks.

The following month the Irish Commission for Justice and Peace approached the British government's Northern Ireland Office with some proposals to end the strikes, while the British Foreign Office held talks with the Provisional IRA. The British government made some concessions but, without agreement, another two strikers died from starvation. In 1981 a striker's family forced him to end his strike, requesting he receive medical attention, but three other strikers died soon after this and another the following month. Five more strikers were given medical attention following their families' request and on 3 October 1981 the strike ended – it had lasted 217 days. Many of the prisoners' rights were restored, including not having to wear prison uniforms.

The strike increased the popularity and strength of Sinn Féin as a political party and it also changed the direction of the IRA, as they began to fight through political means, though they continued their campaign of violence as well. Prior to the hunger strike, middle-class Catholics rarely voted Sinn Féin but the hatred that people felt for Margaret Thatcher in Northern Ireland because of her treatment of their political prisoners solidified Sinn Féin's recognition as a political party. As well as ten hunger strikers, outside the prison 61 people lost their lives in those same months, including 26 members of the security forces killed by the IRA.

MODERN IRELAND

While Northern Ireland was in the midst of the Troubles, the Republic was evolving. In 1973 both the UK and Ireland joined the European Economic Community (EEC). The EEC had a substantial beneficial effect on the Republic, as the subsidies it offered enabled the country's economy to grow. Meanwhile, the economy of Northern Ireland was failing. The tensions were growing and in 1972 London took direct control of Northern Ireland, again, as the Stormont Parliament was suspended. London tried to establish peace talks and to set up a power-sharing executive but both efforts failed. The atrocities committed meant that industry was incapable of flourishing and unemployment skyrocketed. The UK, with the aid of the EEC, pumped in money but, as the fighting continued, the country was unable to find its feet and it remained in an economic recession for nearly two decades.

The violent attacks of the Troubles continued with bombings and segregation by religion until the late 1990s.

EMIGRATION IN THE 1980S

Ireland had three general elections within 18 months in the early 1980s and the country stagnated. Politically, it was very conservative because of a strong religious community and a predominant older population, as many of the young were leaving.

During the 1980s Ireland was, once again, in a deep economic recession. Emigration, which had always been present, once again soared and affected a wide range of people, including the unskilled, semi-skilled and graduates, who were leaving to find opportunities abroad. The numbers show a stark picture: in 1980 only 8 per cent of university graduates left but by 1989 the number had risen to 30 per cent.

DID YOU KNOW?

Emigration in the 1980s is commonly called 'the brain drain'.

ANGLO-IRISH AGREEMENT

In 1985 Garret FitzGerald, the Taoiseach at the time, and Prime Minister Thatcher approved the Anglo-Irish Agreement, which gave Ireland a consulting role in the affairs of Northern Ireland. It was the first negotiation between Britain and Ireland since the Treaty establishing the Irish Free State in 1921 and it marked a considerable advance in the relationship between the two countries. It was decided that any changes to the sovereignty of

Northern Ireland would have to be approved by a vote by its people. The governments hoped that by working together there would be a better chance to bring peace to the North.

FAMOUS FIGURES
CHARLES HAUGHEY (1925-2006)

Charles James Haughey (known as Charlie) was the fourth leader of Fianna Fáil, the conservative party founded by Eamon de Valera. Haughey was Taoiseach three times: 1979–1981, in 1982 and again 1987–1992. His father was in the original IRA and Haughey was tried twice in 1970 for conspiracy to procure arms for the IRA (using government funds); the first trial was aborted and he was acquitted in the second. He was a staunch republican and spoke out in support of the hunger strikers in Northern Ireland. He continued to be linked to several scandals and people began to accuse him of using his connections to the police to intimidate those who went against him. In the 1980s, Haughey resigned after being implicated in an allegation of wiretapping two journalists, both of whom had written critically of him. He stayed away from the spotlight until 1997, when a tribunal proved that he had received large amounts of money from a prominent businessman while he was Taoiseach. After another tribunal investigated his earnings and uncovered a host of other corruptions, he agreed to pay more than €6 million in taxes and penalties.

CELTIC TIGER

By the mid-1980s the government had started to tackle the economic issues. They introduced tough spending restraints and negotiated partnerships that would bring in businesses in return for income tax concessions. This new influx of money from business, coupled with EU funding, enabled Ireland's economy to grow. By the 1990s the EU had given millions to Ireland and changed the face of Irish infrastructure. For the first time in centuries the flow of emigration was reversed: Ireland had become one of the richest nations in the world. By 2000, the need for growth had ended but, regardless, the growth continued. The construction industry, in particular, experienced a boom and property prices soared. Prior to this era, Irish exports buoyed economic growth but this time Ireland's main economic driver rested with the construction industry.

DID YOU KNOW?

Divorce was legalised in Ireland in 1996. A referendum was held in 1995 where 50.3 per cent of the population voted in favour, narrowly winning the vote. There was a 61 per cent voter turnout.

GOOD FRIDAY AGREEMENT

In 1997 the IRA restored their ceasefire (after two previous failed attempts), and republican and loyalist paramilitaries sat down to discuss prospects for peace. Both sides had factions who were opposed to the talks, slowing all progress. In 1998 talks nearly ceased entirely when members of the Ulster Defence Association (UDA) incarcerated in the Maze prison voted in favour of withdrawing from the negotiations with republican paramilitaries. Mo Mowlam – secretary for Northern Ireland (representative of the British government in Northern Ireland) – without consulting the Prime Minister visited the prison and listened to the inmates, promising to address their concerns, and ensured they would offer their support for the talks. Her quick action meant that the talks could continue.

In early 1998 the Ulster Democratic Party and Sinn Féin voluntarily left the negotiations (before being pushed out) in response to killings by their paramilitary factions. This stalled negotiations but the chair of the talks, US Senator George Mitchell, set an end date for 7 April 1998, hoping that a strict deadline would force both sides to start working together. At half past midnight on the night of the deadline, Mitchell presented a 65-page draft agreement but it was rejected by the unionist parties. At this point Tony Blair, Prime Minister of the UK, and Bertie Ahern, Taoiseach of the Republic of Ireland, joined the meeting at Stormont. In the early hours of Good Friday, both sides agreed terms for peace, including nullifying the Irish Constitution's stated claim to Northern Ireland, setting up the Northern Ireland Assembly, plans to decommission weapons and the possibility of early release for paramilitary prisoners.

Two referendums were held on 22 May 1998: one in the Republic of Ireland to ratify the change to the constitution and one in Northern Ireland on whether to accept the terms of the 'Belfast Agreement' (Good Friday Agreement). In the Republic 94 per cent of people voted to cease any claim to Northern Ireland and 71 per cent of those in Northern Ireland voted to accept the terms of the agreement.

DID YOU KNOW?

David Trimble and John Hume shared the Nobel Peace Prize in 1998 for their work on the Good Friday Agreement, the official ceasefire between nationalists and unionists in Northern Ireland.

LGBT+ HISTORY

The first notable campaign for LGBT+ rights began in the 1970s when David Norris, a lecturer in English at Trinity College, Dublin, led the movement to amend the Offences Against the Persons Act 1861. The Act contained a clause that outlawed 'buggery' and in 1977 Norris started legal proceedings to decriminalise homosexuality by repealing it. In 1979 the National Gay Federation (NGF) was established and its building became the hub for the gay community, as well as a place of solidarity. Norris's case went through the courts but was defeated. In 1982 Declan Flynn was beaten and murdered by a group of four people who openly admitted in court to 'gay bashing'. After they received suspended sentences people marched against the verdict. This is considered the first Gay Pride march, and it was aimed at raising awareness of violence against gay men and women. It was the first march in Ireland when the gay community had significant support from the heterosexual community.

In 1988 David Norris, by then a senator, won in the European Court over the constitutional status of the state's criminalisation of certain homosexual acts, and the laws were finally changed in 1993. In 2010, the Civil Partnership Bill was passed, giving more rights than previously to same-sex couples and paving the way for a referendum in 2015, which legalised same-sex marriage in Ireland.

DID YOU KNOW?

Ireland was the first country in the world to legalise same-sex marriage by popular vote.

REFUGEES AND IMMIGRATION

Ireland's long history of emigration finally reversed in the 1990s, with the first large influx of people returning to Ireland as well as those seeking asylum. The population of the country increased exponentially in just over a decade. The speed of economic growth in Ireland created an immediate demand for labour and the largest group of immigrants in the 1990s were Irish nationals returning after years of working abroad.

Asylum applicants also increased in the 1990s; their numbers peaked in the period 2002–2004 and then stabilised. Ireland's citizenship laws were tightened between 2003 and 2005, primarily to eliminate Irish-born children's automatic right to Irish citizenship even if their parents were not Irish citizens. Prior to these rules, parents of a child born in Ireland could receive Irish citizenship based on their child's nationality, leading to fears that non-Irish nationals were purposely giving birth in the country to gain citizenship.

Though the number of asylum applicants lowered from 2004, Ireland experienced mass immigration, driven by the nationals of the new EU nations. After the EU expanded in 2004, Ireland had an influx from citizens of the European Economic Area (EEA) due to their policy of free border movement which allows all EEA nationals the right to live and work anywhere within the EEA. Prior to 2004, work permits in Ireland were largely controlled by employers rather than the State and this had created a rise in non-EEA nationals working in low-skilled occupations in sectors such as agriculture, catering, and so on. However, with the influx of EEA citizens and no means to control numbers through national immigration policy, the government created a list of occupations that became ineligible for work permits (clerical staff, childcare workers, builders, etc.), thus ensuring that preference was given to EEA and Irish citizens. The Employment Permits Act 2006 enacted the reduction of the amount of work permits issued in Ireland and also attempted to enable employers to welcome highly skilled non-EEA workers by offering permanent residency to anyone earning over €60,000 and easy transfers within large companies. This was intended to combat issues of over-population, which turned out to be unnecessary, as recession hit the country and emigration rose again.

DID YOU KNOW?

Mary Robinson became the first female President of Ireland in 1990. She campaigned for divorce, abortion, and LGBT+ and women's rights. She continues to be an advocate for human rights in Ireland and abroad.

RYAN REPORT AND ABUSES OF THE CATHOLIC CHURCH

The Ryan report (previously the Lafoy report, though Mary Lafoy resigned in 2003, citing the Department of Education's refusal to hand over requested documentation) contained the findings by the Commission that investigated the child abuses that took place in more than 250 Church-run institutions. The abuses happened from the 1930s to the 1990s and were particularly prevalent in industrial schools, reformatories, orphanages and hostels. These institutions were filled with children and young adults who were considered negative influences on society for actions such as petty theft and teenage pregnancy. The abuses included chronic beatings, molestation, rape and humiliation. The revelations began in the 1990s and more cases of abuse continue to be reported even today. The Ryan report took nine years to collate and showed that the Church was involved in covering up the atrocities that were being enacted and further exacerbated by the system of sending accused offenders to other institutions where the sexual and physical abuse continued. Having collected evidence from over 1,000 survivors, the report found that the Church showed a general lack of consideration for the safety of children. Many of them considered the report a failure, as the identities of the abusers were kept private (including those already found guilty) and it only led to eight convictions.

In 2010, after it emerged that Cardinal Sean Brady, then head of the Irish Catholic Church, had been present at meetings in 1975 where children were forced to sign vows of silence over their complaints against a paedophile priest, Pope Benedict XVI apologised to Irish survivors.

RECESSION

By 2003 the property boom was largely being funded by foreign borrowing by the banks. The government continued to offer low taxes to large companies, and the Irish economy became reliant on these businesses, as well as the construction boom. Although workers began to demand wage increases, which eroded Ireland's competitive prices within the international economic community, the country remained an attractive destination for foreign direct investment due to the generous tax concessions available. Ireland was enjoying the Celtic Tiger era: finally affluent, people were returning from abroad to work, enjoy life and spend liberally. A thriving arts scene (aided by a tax concession for artists) made Ireland a fun 'young' destination for tourists. However, the economically overheated good times could not last forever, and in 2006 the property bubble finally burst, setting off a reversal in both prices and business activity. This in turn caused huge financial crises amongst the banks. Recession advanced within Ireland but as the global crisis took hold, the country's economy plummeted further than anticipated. In September 2008 Ireland became the first country in the eurozone to enter into recession. In 2010 Ireland was given an €85 billion bailout.

DID YOU KNOW?

In 2002 Ireland changed currency from the pound to the euro.

EMIGRATION (AGAIN)

By 2008, as the global recession hit, emigration increased as the young left the island to find work across the globe. In 2009 the work permit system was once again tightened: it no longer allowed non-EU work permits for jobs earning under €30,000, and required spouses and dependants of non-EU work permit holders to apply for their own work permit rather than having the immediate right to work, as before. The numbers continued to increase as the recession took hold and by 2012 emigration reached a record high only previously seen in the 1980s. Unemployment increased from 4.5 per cent (January 2007) to 15.1 per cent (January 2012), though the numbers were even more severe amongst the youth, where unemployment increased from 9.9 per cent to 33 per cent. The rate of emigration began to fall in 2014, as Ireland emerged from the recession, though by that point another generation had entered the permanent diaspora of the Irish abroad.

ENVIRONMENTAL ISSUES

As elsewhere across the world, Ireland has felt the effects of climate change: the country is warming up and frosty days are decreasing. Although Ireland is subject to EU environmental law, which has raised the profile of environmental issues, it is behind most other EU nations in its role to protect the environment, failing to meet targets to reduce greenhouse gas emissions. Projections estimate that Ireland will miss the 2020 target by 10 per cent and is also behind in terms of protecting natural habitats, specifically peat bogs. Turf cutting has been a popular pastime for generations in summer months, with the cut turf being dried and then used throughout the year for heating.

Since EU legislation protects peat bogs, as an endangered form of biodiversity, turf cutting was banned in 56 bogs throughout Ireland in 2010 and 2011, but in practice it continues almost unchecked.

Ireland now recycles almost 30 per cent of household waste but still lags behind other European countries. That said, recycling has vastly improved: although in 1995 a staggering 92 per cent of municipal waste went to landfill, by 2013 that had fallen to 42 per cent. Despite the dismal results in water usage and biodiversity, Ireland does display a commitment to the environment: its air quality ranges from good to fair and it's the only strand of EU environmental law that the nation is on track with.

IRISH TRAVELLING COMMUNITY

The Irish Travelling community is a nomadic ethnic minority within Ireland. There are an estimated 30,000 Irish Travellers in Ireland and the community can be traced back to the twelfth century. They identify as 'Pavee' or 'Mincier', which are words from their language, Shelta, or the Cant. Though they have social parallels with the Gypsy community, there are no ethnic links. Up until the 1960s the vast majority of Travellers lived in brightly painted wooden horse-drawn caravans or in tents but nowadays these have been replaced with modern mobile homes. Most members live in houses, many taking to the roads in the summer months.

Travellers fought for decades to be acknowledged as a minority ethnicity within Ireland, in hope that this recognition might put an end to discrimination and improve their living conditions. Finally, they were officially legally recognised as an ethnic minority in March 2017.

Culturally, the Irish Travellers are traditionally defined by their nomadic lifestyle. This influenced their employment choices in the past, when they worked as tin-smiths (from where the derogatory name 'tinker' derives), horse traders and seasonal labourers. After World War Two, the community suffered economically due to rural depopulation, farm mechanisation and plastic goods, which made their traditional crafts and skills redundant. This affected their means to earn, sending many of them to live in social housing and becoming dependent on the state for support while others supplemented their income by illegal means.

Many Travellers continued to live traditionally by adapting their skills to the market, such as collecting scrap metal and selling goods door to door. Anti-trespass legislation introduced in the early 2000s further hindered the traditional Traveller way of life, as they could be 'forced on' from the side of roads or any council-owned land. The community has strong family ties, intensified by their disconnection from the settled population. They are also largely devout Catholics and there is a tendency to presume that this is without exception, even though younger Travellers, much like their settled contemporaries, are less religious than previous generations.

Discrimination against Travellers in Ireland is endemic. Irish Travellers are subject to much derision from the settled community, whose tendency to regard the entire group as lawbreakers (and various worse labels) is both common and usually unquestioned. Although 84 per cent of Travellers are unemployed, many of those who are employed hide their background when applying for jobs, thus skewing the statistics.

Their difficult living conditions, which are commonly blamed on the Travelling community, clearly affect their health and well-being: a Traveller man's life expectancy is 15 years lower than that of a settled man (11 years lower for a Traveller woman) and suicide rates are seven times higher. In 1963 a government report labelled the community as a problem and identified the solution as absorbing them into the rest of the population, essentially aiming to obliterate their customs and heritage. More recently, a National Traveller and Roma Inclusion Strategy (2016–2020) is in preparation. It will look to aid Travellers in receiving equal access to healthcare, education and housing. It will also address engagement between the Traveller and settled communities.

ABORTION

Campaigns for abortion in Ireland continue, though it remains illegal (with some exceptions) and is a criminal offence under the 1861 Offences Against the Person Act, which carries a 14-year jail term. In 1983, Ireland held a referendum on the Eighth Amendment to enshrine and protect abortion law in the constitution, in hopes that it could not be altered in the courts (influenced by Roe v. Wade, where the US Supreme Court decided the 'right to privacy' extended to a woman's decision to have an abortion). A majority of 67 per cent voted in favour to add a clause stating that the right to life of the unborn is equal to the right to life of the mother and that future laws would defend and vindicate that right.

In 1991 the European Court of Justice ruled that abortion was a service and, as such, no member state could prohibit distribution of information. In 1992, a thirteenth and fourteenth amendment were added to the Irish Constitution that permitted women to travel abroad for a termination and to receive information about abortions available abroad. In a case in the same year – Attorney General v. X – a 14-year-old girl (X), pregnant as a result of rape, was taken to court for her attempt to seek an abortion. The court ruled that, due to threat of suicide (which could only be averted by termination), she was entitled to seek an abortion, as her life was equal to the right of the unborn.

Again in 1995 the law was amended, in the Regulation of Information Act, which allowed doctors, advisory agencies and counsellors to give information on abortion services abroad, but only when a woman requested it. They were also required to give details on parenting and adoption (regardless of her wishes) and this exchange of information had to be within the confines of one-to-one counselling.

In 2002, the government put forward a referendum that would roll back the rights to an abortion if a woman was suicidal and it was narrowly rejected by voters, with only 42 per cent turnout.

In 2010 Michelle Harte became pregnant whilst receiving treatment for cancer. Her doctor advised her to terminate the pregnancy but Cork University Hospital refused to perform an abortion, as they judged that her life was not in immediate danger. She travelled to the UK to have a termination, while severely ill, and died from cancer in 2011. In the same year the Committee of Ministers of the Council of Europe put pressure on Ireland to address their abortion law, including implementing the right to a termination when a woman's life is at risk.

In 2012 the ambiguous wording of the law was again highlighted when Savita Praveen Halappanavar attended Galway University Hospital while suffering from a miscarriage. Despite her and her husband's requests for a termination, she was refused an abortion because a foetal heartbeat was detectable. She died of septicaemia. Later a report found that her death had been caused by an over-emphasis on the need not to intervene until the foetal heartbeat had stopped and an under-emphasis on managing the risk of infection and sepsis. Pro-choice campaigners, including Savita's husband and mother, called on the government to repeal the Eighth Amendment. In an effort to quell the outcry, the Protection of Life During Pregnancy Act was signed into law in

2013, permitting an abortion if the life of the mother is in danger from physical illness, during an emergency or if there is a clear risk of suicide.

The Protection of Life During Pregnancy Act 2013 was criticised, as it discriminates against any woman who doesn't have the means to travel abroad, by the UN Human Rights Committee, which also urged the Irish government to change the laws and bring them in line with human rights standards. The following year the UN Committee on Economic, Social and Cultural Rights criticised Ireland's abortion law and called for Ireland to hold a referendum for its repeal. Between 2012 and 2016 seven Private Members Bills were put forward to the Dáil to amend Irish abortion law but all of them have been rejected.

In 2016, Taoiseach Enda Kenny said that there would not be a referendum on the Eighth Amendment within the lifetime of his government. The pro-choice campaign has remained active and is gaining traction both in Ireland and abroad, particularly in London, providing information and support to women seeking safe, legal abortions. Every day 11 women must travel from the Republic of Ireland and Northern Ireland to Britain to have a termination.

FAMOUS FIGURES
MICHAEL D. HIGGINS (1941-)

Michael Daniel Higgins is, at the time of writing, the current president of Ireland. He is one of the most popular presidents in the country's history and holds the record for the most votes received by any candidate in an Irish presidential election. The first president to have served as both a member of the Dáil and the Seanad, he is a poet, sociologist, author and broadcaster, as well as a politician. He also lectured in sociology and political science in his youth.

He speaks both Irish and English, and is fluent in Spanish. After his inauguration he requested that his salary be reduced by 23.5 per cent, in line with the cut that his predecessor, Mary McAleese, took after the financial crisis. He has spoken out against homophobia and racism, and throughout his career has campaigned for human rights in Ireland and across the globe.

PORTRAIT OF A PROVINCE: LEINSTER

Leinster is the eastern province of Ireland and comprises 12 counties; its flag is a golden harp on a green backdrop. Originally, Leinster was a small territory of the Laigin (pronounced 'line') tribe. Later, it combined with Mide (modern-day parts of Cavan, Dublin, Kildare, Longford, Louth and Offaly), Osraige (modern-day Kilkenny and Laois) and the Viking settlements of Wexford and Dublin. Though none of the Irish provinces have specific functions on a governmental level (local governments are divided by county), it is still a recognised subdivision of Ireland. Most sports are divided on a provincial level, with Leinster having, inter alia, GAA Hurling and Gaelic football championships, golf club championships and a notable rugby team.

CARLOW - CEATHARLACH

Nickname: The Dolmen County, the Scallion Eaters

Carlow is the second smallest county in Ireland. Its name derives from the old Irish word *cethrae*, a collective term for farmed animals. The settlement of Carlow town is older than written history. Carlow has several examples of megalithic tombs (hence their nickname). One of the finest examples, Brownshill Dolmen, has the largest capstone in Europe. The river Barrow flows through the county and is the official border between Carlow and Laois. The river Slaney also runs through Carlow.

FAMOUS FIGURES
JOHN TYNDALL (1820-1893)

John Tyndall, the nineteenth-century physicist, was from Leighlinbridge in Co. Carlow. His work on magnetism, radiation and gases proved the greenhouse effect. He also confirmed germ theory and that ozone is an oxygen cluster; his hobby of mountaineering led him to further theories of glacier motion and as a result several mountains and glaciers have been named after him (e.g. the Tyndall Glacier, Chile and Mount Tyndall, California). He was an outspoken supporter of Charles Darwin and actively tried to distance religion and science. He became wealthy thanks to his books, lectures, patents and investments, and he gave a lot of the money to science charities, as well as substantial amounts to the Irish Unionist political cause.

DUBLIN – ÁTHA CLIATH

Nickname: The Dubs, the Jacks

Song: 'Molly Malone' or 'Rare Auld Times'

Dublin city is the capital of Ireland and a primate city, meaning it is the political and economic centre of a country (primate cities have at least double the population of the next biggest city in the country). Built by Vikings on the mouth of the river Liffey, it became the capital of Ireland under Norman control. The origin of the name comes from *Dubh*, meaning 'black', and *Linn*, meaning 'pool'. It was a reference to the tidal pool where the river Poddle joined with the river Liffey. Átha Cliath is a gaelicised version of the Viking name, meaning 'ford of hurdles'. As the nation's capital, it is home to the Irish President, the Dáil Éireann, the lower house of government, and Seanad Éireann, the upper house.

DID YOU KNOW?

The lion roaring at the beginning of MGM films was filmed in Dublin Zoo in 1919.

KILDARE – CILL DARA

Nickname: The Lilywhites

Song: 'The Curragh of Kildare'

Kildare County is named after Kildare town but its capital is Naas. Cill Dara translates as 'church of oak', after the monastery founded by St Brigid. The rivers Boyne, Liffey and Barrow run through Kildare, as well as the Royal Canal. This is home to the nature reserve Pollardstown Fen, a popular site for birdwatching and nature enthusiasts. It is also the home of the National University of Ireland, Maynooth, which is known for its music and theology courses. Kildare is also famous for the Japanese Gardens at the Irish National Stud Farm, which are reputed to be the best in Europe.

DID YOU KNOW?

The famous folk singer Christy Moore is from Kildare.

KILKENNY - CILL CHAINNIGH

Nickname: The Cats

Kilkenny County is named after the city, which in turn was named after Cainnech, a medieval abbot who founded the church around which the settlement grew. The county was formerly the kingdom of Osraige. The rivers Barrow, Suir and Nore – often called the three sisters – flow through the county. Kilkenny is famous for hurling and has won more All-Ireland championships than any other county. The team also holds the record for the longest undefeated run, winning 21 consecutive games from 2006 to 2010, when they lost to Tipperary at the All-Ireland final. Kilkenny is renowned for Kilkenny marble: a black marble that has been used for various notable buildings, as well as the plinth of Richard III's tomb and Daniel O'Connell's headstone.

FAMOUS FIGURES
LADIES OF LLANGOLLEN (ELEANOR CHARLOTTE BUTLER, 1739–1829, AND SARAH PONSONBY, 1755–1831)

Eleanor Butler, daughter of the Earl of Ormond, famously fell in love with Sarah Ponsonby, the orphaned child of nobles. The two women met when Eleanor visited Sarah's school and they maintained contact. Once Sarah finished her studies, she spent a lot of time in the nearby Kilkenny Castle, Eleanor's home. As they reached marriageable age, the two women ran off together. They were found sleeping in a barn, dressed as men, and subsequently barred from seeing each other. Shortly after this, Sarah wrote to Eleanor, asking her to come to her. She hid Eleanor in a cupboard in her home but again they were found out. This time, they stood up to their families and booked a boat to England. They settled near Llangollen, in Wales, where they entertained many of the most famous names of the time, including William Wordsworth, Percy Shelley, Lord Byron, Anne Lister and Caroline Lamb. They lived together for 50 years and died within two years of each other. They are both buried at the churchyard in Llangollen.

LAOIS – LAOIS

Nickname: O'Moore County

Song: 'Lovely Laois'

Laois's name is derived from the Loígis kingdom, though modern-day Laois is much smaller. The river Nore goes through the southwest of the county and the river Barrow runs along the east. Before the Irish War of Independence, it was called the Queen's County in honour of Mary I of England. This remains its legal name, as it was never officially changed, though is rarely used. The tower at Timahoe is famous for its Romanesque carved doorway, which is unique amongst Irish round towers. Fionn mac Cumhaill, the legendary leader of the Fianna, is supposed to have hailed from Laois.

DID YOU KNOW?

Laois is the only county that has the same name in English and Irish.

LONGFORD – LONGFORT

Nickname: Slashers

Longford County was named after the Viking town and translates as 'ship's port'. It was originally part of Connacht but James I of England and VI of Scotland transferred it to Leinster in 1608. Longford town is built on the banks of a tributary of the river Shannon, called the river Camlin. As a central town, it is an important hub for many amenities in the Midlands. During the Great Famine, the river Shannon at Drumlish was used to support a corn mill that helped to sustain locals. Drumlish Mill was in business until the 1950s.

DID YOU KNOW?

Francis E. 'Frank' Butler – the exhibition shooter and husband and manager of Annie Oakley – was from Longford.

LOUTH – LÚ

Nickname: The Wee County

County Louth is named after a small village, not far from Drogheda, which took its name from Lugh, the Celtic god. It is the setting to the epic Irish tale of *The Cattle Raid of Cooley (Táin Bó Cúailnge)* where Cú Chulainn protected Ulster (Louth was part of Ulster up until the late sixteenth century) from Queen Meadhbh of Connacht. The 1798 Rebellion was masterminded from Louth, with many of the leaders coming from there, though they were betrayed and subsequently hanged.

DID YOU KNOW?

Louth is the smallest but also the most densely populated county in Ireland.

MEATH – MÍ

Nickname: The Royal County

Song: 'Beautiful Meath'

The name Meath comes from the old Irish *Midhe*, which meant 'middle'. County Meath is steeped in history, and is home to the famous passage tombs at Knowth, Dowth and Newgrange. The Hill of Tara in central Meath was traditionally the seat of the High King of Ireland. Kells is home to the Columban monastery that created the Book of Kells and the five high crosses. In 1935 the Irish Land Commission offered land and a basic farming set-up to entice Gaeilgeoirs (Gaelic speakers) to settle in Meath, in an attempt to revive the Irish language. The offer was taken up by 41 families from Connemara who settled in Ráth Chairn. Later, more families joined and settled in the nearby Baile Ghib. Meath is the only county in Leinster to have a Gaeltacht (Gaelic-speaking) area.

DID YOU KNOW?

Pierce Brosnan was raised in Navan, Co. Meath.

DID YOU KNOW?

The family home of Arthur Wellesley (the Duke of Wellington, who defeated Napoleon at the Battle of Waterloo) was Dangan Castle, in Meath.

OFFALY – UA FÁILGHE

Nickname: The Faithful

Song: 'The Offaly Rover'

County Offaly received its name from the Kingdom of Uí Failghe, though it has little territorial similarity with its namesake. During British reign, it was known as King's County after Mary I's husband, Philip II of Spain. As with County Laois, this name has never formally been changed and sometimes still appears on legal papers. There are several peat bogs in Offaly and some of the greatest archaeological finds have been unearthed there. The largest collection of Bronze Age items was found at Dowris, Co. Offaly.

DID YOU KNOW?

Birr Castle still houses the great telescope, once the largest telescope in the world.

DID YOU KNOW?

Tullamore had the first known aviation disaster. In 1785 a hot air balloon crashed and caused a large fire, destroying two streets. Prior to this incident, the streets had been dilapidated and after they were rebuilt, they enabled Tullamore to become a vibrant trading town.

WESTMEATH – IARMHÍ

Nickname: Lake Men

The Kingdom of Meath was split when Walter de Lacy had no male heirs (his son and grandson died before him) and the land was divided between his two granddaughters, Margery and Maud, in 1241. King Henry III arranged the marriages of both women, ensuring that the lands were kept within control of the English Crown. According to Irish mythology, Westmeath is home to Lough Derravaragh where the Children of Lir spent their first 300 years as swans (see p.149).

DID YOU KNOW?

Sean's Bar in Athlone, a town that straddles the counties of Roscommon and Westmeath, is not only the oldest pub in Ireland, but also the oldest one in Europe.

WEXFORD – LOCH GARMAN

Nickname: Model County, Yellow Bellies

Song: 'The Boys of Wexford', 'Boolavogue'

Wexford town was a Viking settlement, which the county is named after. Although the whole of Ireland is rich in history, Wexford stands out for the volume of evidence from prehistoric times, as well as being one of the first places to be converted to Christianity. It was also the first part of Ireland that the Normans invaded in 1169. On 23 October 1641 Wexford stood strong in support for a confederate Ireland and rebelled against the English Crown. Wexford was also a major player in the rebellion of 1798, on which the county song – 'Boolavogue' – is based.

WICKLOW – CILL MHANTÁIN

Nickname: Garden County

Song: 'The Meeting of the Waters'

The town of Wicklow, which gave the name to the county, was established by the Vikings and its name means 'Viking's meadow'. Wicklow is known for its beauty and its nickname is 'garden county'. The Wicklow Mountains are the largest mountain range in Ireland and many small lakes are scattered throughout the county. It has been used in many films, such as *Braveheart* and *In the Name of the Father*, and is the home of Ardmore Studios.

BOOLAVOGUE

At Boolavogue, as the sun was setting
O'er the bright May meadows of Shelmalier,
A rebel hand set the heather blazing
And brought the neighbours from far and near.
Then Father Murphy, from old Kilcormack,
Spurred up the rocks with a warning cry;
'Arm! Arm!' he cried, 'For I've come to lead you,
For Ireland's freedom we fight or die.'

He led us on against the coming soldiers,
And the cowardly Yeomen we put to flight;
'Twas at the Harrow the boys of Wexford
Showed Booky's Regiment how men could fight.
Look out for hirelings, King George of England,
Search ev'ry kingdom where breathes a slave,
For Father Murphy of the County Wexford
Sweeps o'er the land like a mighty wave.

We took Camolin and Enniscorthy,
And Wexford storming drove out our foes;
'Twas at Sliabh Coillte our pikes were reeking
With the crimson stream of the beaten Yeos.
At Tubberneering and Ballyellis
Full many a Hessian lay in his gore;
Ah, Father Murphy, had aid come over
The green flag floated from shore to shore!

At Vinegar Hill, o'er the pleasant Slaney,
Our heroes vainly stood back to back,
And the Yeos at Tullow took Father Murphy
And burned his body upon the rack.
God grant you glory, brave Father Murphy
And open heaven to all your men;
The cause that called you may call tomorrow
In another fight for the Green again.

LANGUAGE

Ireland has two national languages: Irish (or Gaeilge) and English. There are small pockets of the country, called Gaeltachts, which speak Irish as their first language. Irish is compulsory throughout school, though few people speak or engage with it at all. Linguists divide the language into five periods: primitive (AD 300–500), old (500–950), middle (950–1200), early modern (1200–1750s) and modern Irish (from the 1750s to the present). The Irish language is usually divided into three iterations: Primitive Irish, Middle Irish and Modern Irish.

The majority of the country speaks English, though a peculiar form of English specific to the island is called Hiberno-English, a reference to its Hibernian influence. This language, at times, is unrecognisable from the formal English taught as a foreign language across the world. Many of the differences between Standard English and Hiberno-English have been informed by the Irish language and others by Irish culture.

PRIMITIVE IRISH

Gaeilge Ársa (pronounced 'Gayle-geh Or-sa') or Primitive Irish is the oldest form of Irish. It derived from Goidelic, the Celtic language that is the root of Scots Gaelic (spoken in Scotland) and Manx (spoken on the Isle of Man). It was written in Ogham (pronounced 'Oh-um'), from the third to the sixth century, to mark graves. Most Ogham was written vertically (carved into stone) from bottom to top, though some manuscripts existed where it was written from right to left. There are 20 letters in the alphabet, each one comprising a line or multiple lines that intersected a vertical axis, either horizontal or at an angle. Sometimes the vowels were recorded as dots rather than lines. There are no works of literature in Ogham, and it is only found as inscriptions on otherwise undecorated pillars. After the sixth century, Old Irish was written in the Roman alphabet.

OLD AND MIDDLE IRISH

Around the year AD 500, Primitive Irish evolved into Old Irish, which in turn began to develop into Middle Irish from around AD 900 until 1200. The language had some Scandinavian influence, with words like *pingin* (penny), *bord* (table) and *margadh* (market) being added. There are many manuscripts from both of these eras, though Middle Irish became synonymous with Irish culture, as it was the language used by monks recording Irish prayers, histories, genealogies, legends and myths. Middle Irish began to decline with the arrival of the Normans at the end of the twelfth century.

MODERN IRISH

Ireland was briefly multilingual when the Normans arrived, though by the sixteenth century most of the people on the island were native Irish speakers. Early Modern Irish co-existed with Classical Modern Irish, though the latter was a language being developed by scholars and poets and the former was the language spoken by the majority. English was the formal language used in all administrative and legal positions, preventing the Irish-speaking poor from accessing functional roles in the running of the country. English became more common throughout Ireland in the 1500s due to the Tudor conquest, though Irish remained the language spoken by the majority. When the Penal Laws were relaxed, a greater proportion of the country began to speak English in order to achieve upward social mobility. After the Great Famine the Irish language was nearly lost completely.

By the start of the twentieth century, scholars became interested in the language, its literature and its dwindling population of native speakers. The Gaelic League (*Conradh na Gaeilge*) was established in 1893 to promote Irish. They standardised the language to make it easier to learn and in 1900 they introduced it to primary schools, though it was optional. They ran Irish classes throughout Ireland, including the Gaeltacht areas, where they focused on teaching native speakers how to read and write their language. When the Irish Free State was established, the Irish language was declared the national language of the country and learning Irish became compulsory throughout primary and secondary schooling.

HIBERNO-ENGLISH

Hiberno-English is a variety of English that is used in Ireland. It has developed from the Irish language and is strongest in Gaeltacht areas. It borrows pronunciation, syntax and vocabulary from Irish.

Examples:
Pronunciation: Pronouncing 'sl', 'st' and 'sn' isn't possible in the Irish language, which is why Irish people add a 'h' sound. This is particularly strong in Connemara and Wes(h)t Limerick.

'I want shteak!'

Syntax: The Irish language has no words for 'yes' or 'no': you can only affirm or deny. This has seeped into Hiberno-English.

'Are you going to the shops?'
'I am.'

'Do I take the next left?'
'You do.'

Nouns: Banshee comes from the Irish *Bean Sidhe*.

Smig, meaning chin (often pronounced 'shmig'), comes from the Irish word *smeig*.

Brogues – the style of shoes – is named after the Irish word for shoe.

Gob is the Irish word for beak.

Shamrock comes from the Irish word *seamróg* – the correct English translation is clover.

WORDS ADDED TO ENGLISH

Lynching. The verb 'to lynch' came from James Lynch Fitzstephen, the mayor of Galway in 1493. After his son Walter had broken the law, James sentenced him to death. When crowds gathered outside their house to prevent the hanging, James returned inside and hanged Walter from the window above. The original meaning referred to a private person taking the law into their own hands, though it later evolved to mean mob law.

Hooligan. The term hooligan was first published in a British newspaper in 1898. It derived from the Irish family name Houlihan, which was commonly used in comic music hall songs and newspapers in the late 1800s to portray drunk and often violent Irish characters.

Phoney. This term is derived from the Irish word for ring, *fainne*. In the nineteenth century 'fawney' became a slang term for fake (arising from a distrust of Irish gold). This term travelled to America, where it became the 1920s term for fake gold rings.

Tory. This term comes from the Irish word *toir*, meaning to pursue. As the majority of Irish highwaymen were dispossessed Irish gentry, the most pursued criminals became synonymous with a group that wanted to conserve the past.

COMMON WORDS AND PHRASES

Grand: Mediocre/All right/OK

Sure he can't even handle an egg!: He's useless

What's the craic?: Any news?

Having the craic: Having a good time

I will, yeah: I won't

Bob's your uncle: Something that can be achieved without effort (it began when Arthur Balfour was promoted to the position of chief secretary for Ireland without any relevant experience and nobody was in any doubt it was thanks to his uncle, Robert Gascoyne-Cecil, being Prime Minister)

Notions: Believing you're better than others, a kind of Irish version of 'keeping up with the Joneses', e.g. 'Daly has notions', that is 'Daly thinks a lot of herself'

Amn't: I was shocked to discover during my research that 'amn't' isn't a word. It means 'am not' and Irish people just contract it differently – in Standard English it would be 'I'm not'.

SHELTA, CANT GAMMON, MINCERTOIREE OR THE CANT

The Irish Traveller language (with various names and dialects) is now becoming more anglicised but evolved from Old Irish, which remains its strongest influence. For many years people believed that the language was simply some form of jargon that was constructed for disguise purposes, though studies in the twentieth century discovered its strong links to Old Irish. The language did develop as a secret language, using back slang (the word for 'kiss' is *gop*, which is the Irish word *pog* backwards), switching consonants (the word for girl, *cailin*, became *laicin*) and altering the initial sounds of words (*gather* means 'father', from the Irish word *athair*). These techniques and many others were used to protect their language, which is still in use today and continues to evolve.

POLISH

The 2011 census proved that Polish was the second most spoken language in Ireland (around 150,000 Poles live there), with Irish dropping its position to third. Uptake of Polish as a Leaving Certificate subject is rising and the Polish government have suggested that the language should be taught in Irish schools. Polish schools are now popular throughout the country, teaching Polish language, history and culture at the weekends, as well as organising activities like scouts and art classes run in Polish.

HOLIDAYS AND CELEBRATIONS

FESTIVALS

It's well known that the Irish enjoy a good party and this manifests itself in the sheer amount of festivals and celebrations in the calendar. At any time of the year there are multiple festivals, ranging from small local affairs to national events of international renown. The following sections list only a few of the most interesting and most popular ones but they don't come even close to being comprehensive.

SPORT

ALL-IRELAND FINALS – SEPTEMBER

The finals for hurling and Gaelic football, the national sports, are held at Croke Park, Dublin, on the first and third weekend in September before crowds of up to 82,300 passionate but very well-behaved spectators. Teams representing each county compete during the preceding three months and for the final Dublin is decorated in the colours of the two remaining teams.

CIRCUIT OF IRELAND RALLY – APRIL

First held in 1931 (then called the Ulster Motor Rally), this is the third oldest car rally in the world. In 2017 the event was meant to be called 'The Circuit Festival' for the first time but the rally was cancelled due to lack of funding.

GALWAY RACE WEEK – JULY/AUGUST

A horse racing festival which started as a two-day event and now stretches to a full week. It was immortalised in W. B. Yeats's poem 'At Galway Races'.

AT GALWAY RACES

Here where the course is,
Delight makes all of the one mind,
The riders upon the galloping horses,
The crowd that closes in behind:
We, too, had good attendance once,
Hearers and hearteners of the work;
Aye, horsemen for companions,
Before the merchant and the clerk
Breathed on the world with timid breath.
Sing on: somewhere at some new moon,
We'll learn that sleeping is not death,
Hearing the whole earth change its tune,
Its flesh being wild, and it again
Crying aloud as the racecourse is,
And we find hearteners among men
That ride upon horses.

IRISH DERBY - JUNE/JULY

Every year three-year-old horses race in the Irish Derby, at the Curragh in Co. Kildare – a vast flat land that provides Ireland's most popular flat racing course. The derby's first incarnation (O'Darby Stakes) was in 1817, though that finished in 1824. In 1848 the Curragh Derby was launched but this was also short-lived. The Irish Derby was inaugurated in 1866 by the third Earl of Howth, the third Marquess of Drogheda and the third Earl of Claremont. The event is one of the most popular on the Irish racing calendar.

IRISH GRAND NATIONAL - APRIL

This horse race takes place every Easter Monday at Fairyhouse, Co. Meath. This event, which is for five-year-old horses, has often been won by previous winners of the Irish Derby and by winners of the Grand National (the English equivalent). It was established in 1870 and has run every year except 1919.

LAYTOWN RACES - SEPTEMBER

Among the few horse races that take place on beaches across Ireland, this one in Co. Meath is the only one that follows the Rules of Racing. The first recorded race was – a small – part of the Boyne Regatta in 1868. Though the regatta has long since ceased to take place, the Laytown Races are a popular date on the Irish racing calendar.

MALLOW RACING HOME FOR EASTER FESTIVAL - APRIL

This racing weekend is a little more family-friendly than any of the others (though it still includes standard best-dressed awards, drinking and, of course, horse racing), as it has Easter egg hunts for the children and other events for them to enjoy.

MOURNE INTERNATIONAL WALKING FESTIVAL - JUNE

Walkers of all skill and fitness levels can enjoy the views and trails of the Mourne Mountains in Co. Down over a three-day weekend.

NORTH WEST 200 - MAY

A week-long motorcycle race, this is the largest annual sporting event in Ireland. Confusingly, it takes place on the north coast of Ireland, as the name wasn't changed after the course route between Coleraine, Portrush and Portstewart was chosen.

SIX NATIONS RUGBY - FEBRUARY

Though not technically a festival, the atmosphere when six nations compete against each other in Ireland is certainly akin to one. The Aviva Stadium, Lansdowne Road, in Dublin is relatively central and revellers (with and without tickets) celebrate in the city centre before and after each Ireland match.

MUSIC

CASTLEPALOOZA AND INDIEPENDENCE - JULY/AUGUST

These two small musical festivals take place on the same weekend and often share artists. Castlepalooza takes place in the woods of Charleville Castle, Co. Offaly, in the Midlands, whereas Indiependence is in the south, in Mitchelstown, Co. Cork. The festivals host music, burlesque, comedy, fortune-telling and art exhibitions.

CORK INTERNATIONAL
CHORAL FESTIVAL – MAY

The clue is in the title for this one. This choral festival has been held every year since 1954 in Cork over the May bank holiday weekend. Choirs from all over the world and of all ages take part.

FLEADH CHEOIL NA HÉIREANN – AUGUST

This is an all-Irish traditional music event. Each entry must win county competitions to qualify and then compete in the festival. The host town changes each year and people from all over the country and from abroad travel to watch the performances.

FLEADH NUA – MAY

This traditional Irish music festival began as a three-day event but now runs for eight days. It celebrates traditional Irish music, dancing and culture in Ennis, Co. Clare.

GUINNESS CORK JAZZ FESTIVAL – OCTOBER

This was inaugurated in 1978 during the October bank holiday. It was Ireland's first jazz festival, originally sponsored by John Player and Sons, though Guinness has sponsored the event since the 1980s.

KILKENNY RHYTHM AND
ROOTS FESTIVAL – APRIL/MAY

Since 1998 the streets and pubs of Kilkenny are taken over by Americana Roots musicians, creating a fascinating way to explore this city.

LONGITUDE - JULY

Taking place in Dublin's Marlay Park, this electric and dance music festival draws in the crowds each year for a fun and exciting weekend.

WEXFORD OPERA FESTIVAL - OCTOBER/NOVEMBER

This festival is well known throughout the opera world for promoting new works, forgotten classics and lesser known operas. It also aims to offer opportunities to upcoming performers. The festival began in 1951, and has steadily grown in size and renown.

WILLIE CLANCY SUMMER SCHOOL - JULY

Also known as Willie Clancy Week, this summer school doubles as a traditional Irish music, song and dance festival in Miltown Malbay, Co. Clare. Willie Clancy was a famous musician who played the uilleann pipes. Lectures, performances and ceilís are held throughout the week.

LITERARY

BLOOMSDAY - JUNE

Bloomsday is a celebration of James Joyce. *Ulysses*, the novel that is generally considered his greatest work, is set on 16 June 1904 and follows the life of Leopold Bloom. In reality 16 June was Joyce's first date with his wife Nora Barnacle. Nowadays, the festival lasts for five days. There are walks around the city that show Joyce's Dublin and the city's literary history, as well as thematically similar pub crawls, readings, music, theatre events and a tour that follows the route of Leopold's day. One of the biggest events is Bloomsday

Breakfast, where people gather, dressed in Edwardian garb, to eat the same breakfast that Leopold had in the book (warning: it contains kidneys!) while dramatic readings from the book are performed.

DID YOU KNOW?

Bloomsday is also celebrated in Szombathely, Hungary, where (the fictional) Leopold's father, Virág Rudolf, was born.

DUBLIN WRITERS WEEK – MAY

The best-known names in literature gather together to discuss, debate and lecture all aspects of literary life and history.

LIMERICK LITERARY FESTIVAL – FEBRUARY

This literary festival is held in honour of Kate O'Brien, a Limerick author (it was originally Kate O'Brien weekend but now runs for four days). It holds an annual competition for best novel or short story collection by a debut female writer and celebrates writers, artists, books and readers.

MIXED ARTS

BARE IN THE WOODS – JUNE

Not a nudist celebration, as the title might have you believe, it stands for 'Bringing Another Righteous Event'. The festival is held in the woods of Garryhinch, Co. Laois, providing three days of music, comedy, spoken word, art installations, games, sports and artisan food.

BELFAST INTERNATIONAL ARTS FESTIVAL – OCTOBER/NOVEMBER

Formerly known as Belfast Festival at Queen's, it was founded in 1962 at the university. It is now held in venues across the city.

CATHEDRAL QUARTER ARTS FESTIVAL – APRIL/MAY

This festival takes place in Belfast and is centred near St Anne's Cathedral, though it now takes place in several venues across the city. It began in 2000 and focused on a socially inclusive billing across all media of the arts.

CLONMEL JUNCTION FESTIVAL – JULY

This nine-day festival starts on the first weekend of July and offers theatre, circus, art, street theatre and music events throughout Clonmel town. Every year local schoolchildren create street art that decorates the town during the festival.

ELECTRIC PICNIC – SEPTEMBER

This is a music and arts festival – one of the most popular festivals in Ireland – which hosts some of the most famous names and developing artists in music as well as other genres of performance. Each year charities host stands that can inform and entertain the festivalgoers. Food at the festival is also considered part of the performance and the 'theatre of food' invites famous names to entertain the public by showcasing their love of food.

FÉILE AN PHOBAIL – AUGUST

Féile An Phobail means 'festival of the people', though the event is also known as the West Belfast Festival. It takes place on the Falls Road in Belfast for two weeks in summer, though two smaller festivals are held during the year – for young people (Draiocht) and a celebration of Irish and Celtic culture (Féile an Earraigh) – as well as several events throughout the year. The festival, which celebrates Irish and international culture, sprang from a series of tragic attacks: in 1988 an Ulster loyalist paramilitary attacked the funeral of an IRA terrorist and killed three mourners. At the funeral of one of them two British officers were killed. The Falls Road became synonymous with terrorism and danger so the festival was started that same year to try to highlight the positive sides of the community.

FÉILE NA BEALTAINE – APRIL/MAY

A festival in Dingle, Kerry, that celebrates all of the arts. Bealtaine was the Celtic holiday of spring, similar to May Day, and takes place traditionally on 30 April or 1 May. This festival, which lasts five days, is well worth a visit – Kerry people know how to throw a party.

GALWAY INTERNATIONAL ARTS FESTIVAL – JULY

This is one of the largest festivals in Ireland. The entire city of Galway celebrates and it feels as if every available space has become a place of performance, discussion, art and spectacle. In a city of just under 80,000, the festival has as many as 165,000 patrons.

KILLARNEY SUMMERFEST – JULY

This family-friendly event (teddy bear picnic, anyone?) takes place over nine days. Famous comedians, rock stars and other musicians gather in Killarney, Co. Kerry, nestled amongst some of the most beautiful scenery in Ireland.

KILKENNY ARTS FESTIVAL - AUGUST

Also known as Kilkenny arts week, this festival began in 1974 and initially focused on classical music. Now it celebrates all of the arts and works as a showcase for artists presenting work across this beautiful medieval city.

OTHER

CAT LAUGHS - JUNE

This comedy festival is held in Kilkenny, southern Leinster. There are no awards or competitions, making it an easy-going event that's proving extremely popular.

DUBLIN FRINGE FESTIVAL - SEPTEMBER

This 16-day fringe theatre (small productions) takes place throughout the centre of the city. It focuses on emerging Irish and international artists across many different performance styles in both traditional and non-traditional venues.

DUBLIN INTERNATIONAL FILM FESTIVAL - FEBRUARY

This young festival was established in 2003 to celebrate great film in the country's capital. The festival was originally sponsored by Jameson but since 2016 has been supported by Audi.

DID YOU KNOW?

Dublin has the highest cinema attendance per capita in the EU.

DUBLIN THEATRE FESTIVAL – SEPTEMBER/OCTOBER

This is Europe's oldest theatre festival, having started in 1957. The standard is very high and it brings world-class performances to Dublin from across the globe, as well as premieres of new works. There are usually big names to be seen throughout.

DURROW SCARECROW FESTIVAL – JULY/AUGUST

Durrow, Co. Laois, has been holding a scarecrow festival since 2009. Despite its recent beginnings, the festival is growing quickly due to the fantastic creations (which are more akin to works of art than a traditional scarecrow) that are dotted throughout the town (and competing in the Scarecrow Championship). There are also crafts, markets and entertainments that add to this fun, novel festival.

GALWAY FILM FLEADH – JULY

Run concurrently with the Galway International Arts Festival, this film festival promotes both foreign and Irish cinema. It hosts conferences, classes and networking events.

GALWAY INTERNATIONAL OYSTER FESTIVAL – SEPTEMBER

This festival celebrates oyster season in Galway. The first one hosted 34 people in one pub but it now holds a range of events over a long weekend.

LISDOONVARNA MATCHMAKING FESTIVAL – SEPTEMBER/OCTOBER

This festival has been taking place during the month of September and often the beginning of October for over 200 years. It is the biggest singles event in Europe and 20,000 people gather in this small town (population 739). Dances are held every day throughout the festival, starting at noon until the early hours of the morning. Many come for the celebration rather than meeting their match, which is fortunate, as there is only one remaining matchmaker in town. Matchmaking is a very old tradition in Ireland that has died out, except in Lisdoonvarna. In the eighteenth century the mineral waters at Lisdoonvarna were considered one of the best places in Ireland to recuperate from rheumatism, glandular fever and other illnesses. It soon became a hot spot for the gentry, who arrived in September because of the good weather and, as they were all gathered in one place, this became a natural hub for setting up marriages. Soon local matchmakers offered to find suitable matches for a fee.

NATIONAL PLOUGHING CHAMPIONSHIP – SEPTEMBER/OCTOBER

Inaugurated in 1931, this festival is now one of the biggest outdoor events in the world. The venue changes each year, ensuring that it visits every county in Ireland. Nearly 300,000 people gather in all weathers, for all manner of events and exhibitions. Aside from the ploughing competition, there are farming and machinery exhibitors, music, dancing, fashion shows, sheep dog trials, games (including a welly toss) and countless other events that combine to create the highlight of the rural social calendar and an impressive hike in the local Irish economy.

PRIDE – JULY

Pride marches and accompanying festivities take place all over Ireland. Dublin hosts the largest parade, while Belfast holds the largest festival. Lisdoonvarna has a matchmaking Pride-infused festival.

PUCK FAIR – AUGUST

Puck Fair is one of Ireland's oldest fairs, counting nearly 400 years of annual celebrations (that is, those that have been recorded but it may well be a lot older, as no one knows how the fair began – or why). On 10–12 August Killorglin, Co. Kerry, becomes a hive of free entertainment. It starts with a group catching a wild goat and naming him King Puck (*puc* is the Irish word for a billy goat). The festivities kick off with a horse fair on the first day and a cattle fair on the second. The pubs stay open till 3 a.m. – a legal exception – and even later if you find the right pub. The town is filled with a host of activities for families – and concerts, dances, events and steady drinking for everyone else.

ROSE OF TRALEE – AUGUST

The Rose of Tralee International Festival is a big celebration that takes the 'roses' (a woman of Irish descent who represents her county or home country in the competition) around Ireland before finally they are interviewed on live television in Tralee, Co. Kerry. Tralee held an annual carnival that elected a carnival queen but this ended after World War Two. In 1957, as a means of improving tourism, they reinstated the pageant but this time they based the title on a local traditional song, 'The Rose of Tralee'. Originally, entrants had to be from Tralee but then it was broadened to Kerry and finally to any woman of Irish birth or ancestry. Nowadays, the 'roses' are selected from all over the globe, and each Irish county, with 32 entrants making the final event. The modern competition focuses on the fact that it is a celebration of Irish culture and not a beauty pageant, as the women are not judged on their appearance but on their suitability to serve as ambassadors for Ireland and fitting the description of the song. The festival also includes a parade of the roses, fireworks, street performance and many other attractions.

ROSE OF TRALEE

The pale moon was rising above
the green mountain,
The sun was declining beneath the blue sea;
When I strayed with my love to
the pure crystal fountain,
That stands in the beautiful Vale of Tralee.
She was lovely and fair as the
rose of the summer,
Yet 'twas not her beauty alone that won me;
Oh no, 'twas the truth in her eyes ever dawning,
That made me love Mary, the Rose of Tralee.

The cool shades of evening their
mantle were spreading,
And Mary all smiling was listening to me;
The moon through the valley her
pale rays was shedding,
When I won the heart of the Rose of Tralee.
Though lovely and fair as the rose of the summer,
Yet 'twas not her beauty alone that won me;
Oh no, 'twas the truth in her eyes ever dawning,
That made me love Mary, the Rose of Tralee.

In the far fields of India, 'mid
war's dreadful thunders,
Her voice was a solace and comfort to me,
But the chill hand of death has
now rent us asunder,
I'm lonely tonight for the Rose of Tralee.
She was lovely and fair as the
rose of the summer,

Yet 'twas not her beauty alone that won me;
Oh no, 'twas the truth in her eyes ever dawning,
That made me love Mary, The Rose of Tralee.

DID YOU KNOW?

Gabby Logan, the sports commentator and TV presenter, was the Leeds Rose in 1991.

ST PATRICK'S DAY – MARCH

Thanks to Ireland's long history of emigration, St Patrick's Day is celebrated all over the world. In Ireland it is a four-day event, with parades taking place in every town in the country on 17 March, which is a National Holiday. In many places there are fireworks displays. Artists create elaborate works and the festival seeks to promote Irish arts, achievements and culture, ensuring that this celebration represents the diverse modern Ireland of today. The principal events are held in central Dublin and only New York has a larger parade.

DID YOU KNOW?

The first St Patrick's Day parade was held in New York City in 1762.

WEST WATERFORD FESTIVAL OF FOOD – APRIL

This festival, which is a must for anyone who loves their food, is about to celebrate its tenth anniversary, and started as a way to promote the local foods from West Waterford and the surrounding area but has become an interactive sharing of ideas, influences, flavours and knowledge from top chefs. The festival hosts a large market as well as foodie bus tours, foraging expeditions, cooking demonstrations and several dining experiences.

CELEBRATIONS

FUNERALS AND WAKES

Pagan traditions lived on in Irish wakes for longer than in most Christian countries and arguably are still active today. Traditionally, when a death occurred, the local women and women of the family would wash the body and lay it out in the largest room of the home. The corpse was covered in white linen and decorated with ribbons (usually black or white), and candles were lit and placed around it. People would arrive and smoke was kept in the room, usually by the men smoking pipes, to hide the body from evil spirits. The clocks were set to the time of death and the mirrors were covered with black cloth. People would drink and celebrate the life of the deceased, sharing stories of their exploits. The body was never left alone until the burial. Women would gather to keen (wailing, slightly high-pitched – thankfully no longer much practised), as well as to read poetry. After three days the body would be placed in a casket and brought outside. Mourners would line up and say (often kiss) goodbye to the deceased. When the final mourner had paid their respects, the coffin was closed. The mourners would then gather behind a cart that carried the coffin (or they would carry it if the church was close enough). Strangers would stop to let the funeral pass and people blessed themselves as a mark of respect. At the church a priest would say a funeral mass and the person would be buried in the graveyard. Afterwards many games and drinking took place – the focus was on celebration.

Today parts of this ceremony still exist. The wake is held the day before the funeral, usually at a funeral parlour – rarely at a pub (though this was regularly practised until very recently) – and the casket is open so people can pay their respects. After the funeral people will move on to a named pub or the home of the next of kin and celebrate the life of the deceased. The wake still centres on food, drink, stories and community, as it is primarily a celebration and a fun occasion. Many would argue they're more fun than a wedding – much of a muchness, I'd say!

AMERICAN WAKE

American Wakes date back to before the Famine, though they became particularly popular during this period, when people would gather to celebrate the life and future of an emigrant. As the distance was so great and the people so poor, emigrating usually meant that this was the last time friends and family would see each other – a virtual death. American Wakes lasted up until the 1950s and today going-away parties are often (jokingly) referred to as an American Wake.

HALLOWE'EN – 31 OCTOBER

Hallowe'en is an Irish tradition that came from the Celtic celebration of Samhain, which marked the end of the harvest season and the beginning of winter. It was believed that at this time the spirits from the otherworld had an easier passage to revisit ours. Traditionally, people would leave out gifts for the spirits to appease them (and save their cattle through the winter months). Feasts would be held where an empty place would be left for deceased loved ones in case they wished to join, and some dressed up in order to avoid the ghosts of their past. Today, as in many places around the world, pranks are played, and children dress up and are given sweets, fruit and nuts. Up until very recently, children made their costumes from different clothes and items in the house but lately they are mainly shop-bought.

THE DAY OF THE WREN – ST STEPHEN'S DAY (26 DECEMBER)

This is an old Kerry tradition that has largely died out, though it can be experienced in some areas of the county. A group of boys would hunt a wren (in more recent years this has been a fake wren for obvious animal welfare reasons). The bird would then be tied to a stick or put in a net while the group, wearing straw masks and suits, went from house to house singing and being given a few coins for their effort. Nowadays, though not common, the group visits various houses, singing and playing instruments as the community gathers together for a session.

WEDDINGS

Obviously, declaring your union publicly isn't limited to Ireland but there are many traditions within the Irish ceremony. One example involves the Infant of Prague: a Catholic statue (of Jesus as a boy, dressed in regalia and holding an orb with a cross) is left outside to guarantee good weather on the day – 100 per cent success rate in my experience!

TRADITIONS

Ireland is full of traditions, many of which are understandably dying out with time. Some continue, usually out of habit or to entertain, though I'm sure there must be a few that are still going strong.

IRISH BLESSINGS

Irish blessings were popular in the nineteenth century and earlier. It was customary to wish someone well as they entered or left your home or the pub, and especially if someone was going on a long journey or experiencing a hard time. Now they are only found printed on various objects and sold in tourist shops. The most well-known was basically wishing someone good luck:

> *May the roads rise to meet you,*
> *May the wind be at your back,*
> *May the sun shine warm upon your face,*
> *The rain fall soft upon your fields,*
> *And, until we meet again,*
> *May God hold you in the palm of His hand.*

CHRISTMAS DIP – CHRISTMAS DAY, 25 DECEMBER

Though this takes place across the country, it primarily happens in Dublin and the most popular spot is the 'Forty Foot' at Sandy Cove. People gather on Christmas Day to jump off the promontory and have a morning swim. Rumours abound that it will cure a hangover, but the customary hot whiskey that is enjoyed after is probably more likely to act as a remedy.

CLADDAGH RINGS

The Claddagh ring, named after the area it hails from in Galway, is a ring that comes from the late 1600s. The design is a heart wearing a crown being held by two hands, representing love and loyalty. How the ring is worn indicates the relationship it signifies or the current relationship status of the wearer.

Right hand, heart tip pointing
outwards: Looking for love
Right hand, tip pointing towards
the heart: Heart is taken
Left hand, tip pointing outwards:
Engaged
Left hand, tip pointing towards
the wearer's heart: married

MAGPIES

At university an Italian friend asked me to explain why in Ireland people wave at certain birds. I stared blankly, assuring her that we do no such thing, but when she mentioned that she had started waving at black-and-white birds so that bad things wouldn't happen, I suddenly had to admit that I was wrong – we do! We wave at a magpie (or some touch their heel) so that we won't have bad luck. (Strangely, waving at birds sounded like a bizarre thing to do but waving at a single magpie... utterly normal.) There is a ditty about magpies that still exists in Ireland and some parts of the UK.

One for sorrow,
Two for joy,
Three for a girl,
Four for a boy,
Five for silver,
Six for gold,
Seven for a secret never to be told.

PROPOSING ON A LEAP YEAR

Traditionally, 29 February was the only day a woman could propose. An American film, *Leap Year*, was centred around this tradition and that fact is about the only thing that rings true within the film. Unsurprisingly, a woman can propose any day of the year now, though radio shows and local papers still report women that propose on 29 February.

WEDDING CAKE UNDER YOUR PILLOW

There was a tradition that bridesmaids or, according to some sources, any women attending a wedding would take home a piece of the wedding cake and sleep with it under their pillow. Apparently, it would make you dream the face of your future husband. Aside from the tradition simply becoming outdated, few wedding cakes are still made of sturdy fruitcake and therefore might just make a mess.

PORTRAIT OF A PROVINCE: MUNSTER

Munster, the southern province of Ireland, has had its name since the early Middle Ages. St Patrick set up a lot of churches there and spent many years in this part of the country. Though Vikings tended to live within their Norse settlements, Munster had quite a few Norse towns, including Cork, Waterford and Limerick. In the twelfth century Munster was divided into three kingdoms – Desmond, Ormond and Thomond – which are represented by the three crowns on the Munster flag.

DID YOU KNOW?

Munster declared itself a republic during the Irish Civil War, though it was not long-lived.

CLARE – CLÁR

Nickname: Banner County

Song: 'My Lovely Rose of Clare'

Originally named County Thomond (until 1565), it is unsure whether Co. Clare was named after the de Clare family or whether the name came from the town of Clarecastle (meaning 'plain castle' in the Irish language). Most of Clare is surrounded by water: Lough Derg to the southeast, the river Shannon to the south, Galway Bay to the north and the Atlantic Ocean to the west. Looking over the Atlantic Ocean are the Cliffs of Moher. Clare is also home to the Burren, a rocky terrain made up of limestone that is famous for its flora and fauna.

DID YOU KNOW?

Most *Father Ted* episodes were filmed in Clare. Today you can visit Ted, Dougal and Jack's parochial house and have afternoon tea there.

THE BURREN

The Burren – anglicised from *boireann*, meaning a stony place – is a harsh landscape of white limestone rock. It is Ireland's smallest national park and the inhospitable site is dotted with hazel trees. There are very few mature trees in the Burren and although the view of the rocks in all directions can make it seem entirely barren, it is, in fact, full of plant life. Archaeological studies have shown that trees such as elm would have grown in the lowlands of the Burren in the Neolithic era but they died out (most likely from elm disease or some other outbreak) and never really grew back (as they did in the rest of Ireland and the UK). The thin covering of soil allows for a surprisingly diverse plant life: the Burren is the only place where alpine, Arctic, Celtic, Scandinavian and Mediterranean plants grow naturally.

CORK – CORCAIGH

Nickname: Rebel County

Song: 'Come Back Paddy Reilly'

Cork County is named after the town, which in turn was clearly named after the land (*corcach* meant 'swamp'). The largest county in Ireland, it has a stunning coastland, boasting a range of cliffs, mountains and beaches. It contains the southernmost tip of mainland Ireland at Brow Head and there are many islands off its coast. Cork was originally nicknamed the 'Rebel County' because of its population's insurgence against the Norman invasion. The name stuck due to the part they played in the English Wars of the Roses – when a group attempted to aid the overthrow of Henry VII (and were executed for their pains) – and lived on through the important role they played in the Irish War of Independence.

DID YOU KNOW?

Kissing the Blarney Stone at Blarney Castle is meant to give you 'the gift of the gab'. The term 'blarney' (meaning chatter, flattery, wit) comes from this stone. It is an extremely popular tourist destination.

KERRY – CIARRAÍ

Nickname: The Kingdom

Song: 'Rose of Tralee'

Kerry means 'people of the Ciar' – or the dark people – and is one of the most popular tourist destinations in Ireland, particularly the Dingle Peninsula and Killarney National Park, as many traditions have been kept alive. Kerry is the most mountainous county and is home to Carrauntoohil, the country's highest peak, as well as the second largest Gaeltacht area in Ireland. Kerry has produced an incredible amount of notable people, such as the politicians Daniel O'Connor and Michael Collins, and artists, such as the playwright John B. Keane and the actor Michael Fassbender.

DID YOU KNOW?

There is a local friendly dolphin called Fungie who lives in and around Dingle harbour and swims over to greet divers, kayakers, surfers, swimmers and boats.

LIMERICK – LUIMNEACH

Nickname: Treaty County

Song: 'Limerick, You're a Lady'

County Limerick is named after the city, which was originally a Viking settlement. There is disagreement about whether the name derives from the Irish, meaning 'bare spot', or evolved from the Viking name that meant 'mighty noise'. The city has experienced many sieges: during the 1641 rebellion, in 1650 – when Oliver Cromwell held the city under siege for a year – and in 1690 and 1691 during the Williamite War.

DID YOU KNOW?

Richard Harris, the actor known for playing Dumbledore in the first two *Harry Potter* films amongst many other roles, was from Limerick.

TIPPERARY – TIOBRAID ARAINN

Nickname: Premier County

Song: 'Slievenamon'

The county is named after Tipperary town, which means 'well of the Arra', after the river. From the late nineteenth century up until 2014 the county was divided into North and South Tipperary. The county is drained by four rivers: the Suir, Shannon, Nore and the Munster Blackwater. Tipperary is the largest landlocked county in Ireland and has several mountain ranges – the Arra Hills, Galtees, the Knockmeandown and the Silvermine Mountains – as well as plains and bogs.

SLIEVENAMON

Alone, all alone, by the wave washed strand
All alone in the crowded hall
The hall it is gay, and the waves they are grand
But my heart is not there at all
It flies far away, by night and by day
To the times and the joys that are gone
I never can forget the sweet maiden I met
In the valley near Slievenamon

It was not the grace of her queenly air
Nor her cheek like the rose's glow
Nor her soft black eyes, nor her flowing hair
Nor was it her lily-white brow
'twas the soul of truth and of melting ruth
And her smile like the summer's dawn
That stole my heart away, one soft summer day

In the valley near Slievenamon

In the festive hall by the star-watched shore
Ever my restless spirit cries
My love, oh my love, shall I ne'er see you more
Oh my land, will you never uprise
By night and by day, I ever, ever pray
While lonely my life flows on
To see our flag unrolled and
my true love to enfold
In the valley near Slievenamon

WATERFORD – PORT LAIRGE

Nickname: The Déise

Song: 'Old Dungarvan Oak'

Waterford is the oldest city in Ireland, having been settled by the Vikings in the ninth century. The name in Irish means 'port of Larag' but Waterford comes from the Norse name for the city, which translates as 'ram's fjord'. Waterford has a small Gaeltacht community at Ring, Sean Phobal and Gaeltacht na nDéise, outside of Dungarvan. The county has many megalithic tombs and Ogham stones. It is also the home of Reginald's Tower in Waterford city, whose construction started in 1003 and is the first brick and mortar building in Ireland.

DID YOU KNOW?

Ernest Walton, the physicist, was from Dungarvan in County Waterford. He and his colleague John D. Cockcroft were the first people to artificially split an atom and they won the Nobel Prize for Physics in 1951 for their work.

RELIGIONS IN THE REPUBLIC OF IRELAND

The role of religion is changing constantly in Ireland. Though the country has a strong tradition of Roman Catholicism, atheism is growing rapidly. In 2011 when asked if religion played a significant part in their life, 52 per cent of Irish people responded, 'No.' Few attend mass or any service regularly and yet many will marry in a church ceremony and baptise their children. The role of the Church has been relegated to tradition, in many cases, rather than belief.

ATHEISM, IRRELIGIOUS AND NON-PRACTICING

In the 2011 census 6 per cent declared that they had no religion. Atheists in Ireland are split amongst those who don't believe in God as a personal belief and campaigners who seek to separate the Church from the state (the Catholic Church still has a strong influence over health and education). In the 2016 census 468,400 people recorded that they had no religion – a 73 per cent rise from 2011. The majority of these people were in the cities, less likely to marry and educated to post-graduate level.

BAPTIST

The Baptist community runs as independent churches throughout the country, though the Association of Baptist Churches in Ireland was set up in 1895 to allow these churches to work together. The earliest known Baptist churches were established in the seventeenth century – the first was in Cork in 1640. In the early 1800s the Baptist Church had a surge, with new churches opening nearly every year. However, after the Irish Famine the numbers depleted.

BUDDHISM

The first Buddhists recorded as resident in Ireland appeared in the 1871 census, though references to the religion can be found in the sixth and seventh centuries. Many Buddhists were involved in the peaceful process for Home Rule. Today Buddhism is Ireland's fourth largest non-Christian religion.

CHURCH OF IRELAND (ANGLICAN)

The Church of Ireland has nearly 400,000 members: two-thirds of them live in Northern Ireland and the other third in the Republic, where it is the second largest Christian Church (it is the third largest in Northern Ireland). It continues to serve the entire island, regardless of political borders. It is an Anglican Church that links to St Patrick's founding church in the fifth century, as the division from Catholicism happened in the sixteenth century. In 1871 the Church of Ireland became self-governing, with its own General Synod.

CHURCH OF JESUS CHRIST OF LATTER-DAY SAINTS (MORMONS)

Followers of the Church of Jesus Christ of Latter-day Saints – more commonly known as Mormons – were first recorded in Ireland in 1840 when an American missionary arrived and formed a branch in County Down. The LDS Church was founded in New York in 1830. In Ireland the community was small and met with a lot of hostility. The majority of the Irish mission emigrated to the US, particularly to Utah, where there was a community already established. A branch was set up in 1850 in Dublin, though this soon decreased so substantially that it was put in the care of the British mission. In 1884 a new branch was set up in Belfast and in 1900 the Dublin branch was re-established. Later in the decade, the Irish members were requested to remain in Ireland, and not to emigrate, in order to build up an Irish mission. The religion grew over the next half-century, with the first church-owned meeting house built in 1953, though to this day there are no Mormon temples in Ireland. The LDS Church currently has nearly 6,000 members in Ireland.

EASTERN ORTHODOXY

Though members of the Orthodox Church lived in Ireland in the early twentieth century, the first parish was established in 1969.

Russians came to Ireland after the 1917 Revolution, bringing their beliefs, but their numbers were so small that they didn't set up a parish. The first Orthodox church was a Russian Orthodox one, though today there are Greek Orthodox, Antiochian Orthodox and Romanian Orthodox churches as well. In the 1990s the number of Orthodox churches increased, as immigration during the economic boom years brought more people to Ireland's shores.

EVANGELICAL

The Evangelical Alliance Ireland was established in 2004 so that the individual evangelical churches would have a national body of support. The community in Ireland is very small, though it grew in popularity during the boom years. Approximately 1.5 per cent of the Irish population are members of the Evangelical Church in Ireland.

DID YOU KNOW?

Ireland has the lowest percentage of Evangelical Christians in the English-speaking world.

HINDUISM

Hinduism is increasing in popularity in the Republic of Ireland and Northern Ireland, though it remains a minor religion. In the Republic the religion has surpassed Buddhism and is the eighth largest one.

ISLAM

Islam arrived in Ireland quite late, though it grew at an extremely fast rate and continues to grow. Today, Islam is Ireland's second largest non-Christian religion. In 1959 a group of students from South Africa, India, Malaysia and various other countries began the Dublin Islamic Society. There was no mosque in Dublin at the time so the students used their homes and rented halls for important holidays. The first mosque opened in 1976 in Dublin and in Cork the Muslim community are raising money to build a new mosque, as they are currently operating out of an industrial site.

JEHOVAH'S WITNESS

There are approximately 6,000 Jehovah's Witnesses in Ireland. Meetings are held in the houses of 'publishers' (members of the Church). The community is very small, though, and also tightly knit.

JUDAISM

In 1079 the first Jews known to visit Ireland arrived. They were most likely merchants and offered gifts to Tairdelback, the king of Munster. Nothing else is known about them other than the fact that they visited and immediately left. A century later Strongbow received financial backing by Josce Jew of Gloucester, who enabled him to travel to Ireland. In 1232, the first sign of a Jewish community can be seen in Ireland, as Peter de Rivall was granted a governing position, including 'the custody of the King's Judaism in Ireland'. There is no substantial information on this Jewish community, including what happened during their expulsion from England in 1290 under King Edward I, though most likely they must have been expelled from Ireland as well.

In 1496, when Jews were expelled from Portugal, a small community settled in the south of Ireland. One of their members became mayor of Youghal, County Cork, in 1955. It is unknown what happened to this community, as later records don't show any Jewish population in Cork (though there was a small community in Dublin in the 1700s). In 1728, a Jewish cemetery was established at Ballybough Bridge; there was a synagogue at Marlborough Green and the community consisted of approximately 200 people. A bill was put forward in the Irish House of Commons in 1746 to naturalise people professing the Jewish religion in Ireland, but George II did not agree. Throughout the 1700s and into the mid-1800s the Jewish community continued to fight for recognition and for their rights. In 1844 the Irish Marriage Act made provisions that protected marriages according to Jewish rites. There was some Jewish immigration into Ireland which increased substantially at the end of the nineteenth century because of the anti-Jewish Russian Pogroms.

DID YOU KNOW?

Daniel O'Connell is best known for his work in getting Catholic emancipation but he also supported the Jewish community in their campaign for rights. He personally worked to repeal the 'De Judaismo' law which prescribed special dress for Jews.

In 1904 many Jewish people left Limerick city because of the Limerick Boycott, when a local priest called for an economic boycott on the Jewish community. One member of his congregation then went out and attacked the local *rebbe*, and was celebrated when he returned home. The mood in the city, being so antagonistic, led to several Jewish families moving away, mostly south to Cork. The action was condemned by the majority of Ireland and Michael Davitt was particularly vocal in his disgust. During the War of Independence many Irish Jews joined the IRA – notably Robert Briscoe, who made a successful deal for arms with Germany.

During World War Two, Ireland disgracefully accepted as few as 30 Jewish refugees; though there were no great anti-Semitic acts during that time, this is largely due to the country's apathy and small Jewish community rather than any goodwill. There were some cases of anti-Semitic attacks and Oliver J. Flanagan, an independent TD, made a speech asking for the expulsion of all Jews from Ireland. During the war the Jewish population counted around 5,500 people but by 2015 the census recorded fewer than 2,000 Jews in Ireland.

LUTHERAN

There is a very small community of Lutherans in Ireland. The Church was established in the seventeenth century after the Battle of the Boyne, when one of the pastors in the English Army was approached by German and Scandinavian merchants who asked him to preach in Dublin. A Lutheran church was built there (and referred to locally as 'the Dutch church') but burned down before World War One. The Lutheran community didn't rebuild it and stopped gathering. The Lutheran Church was re-established in 1955 and today has fewer than 500 registered members, the majority of whom are German-speaking and living in Dublin.

METHODIST CHURCH IN IRELAND

The Methodist Church is the fourth largest Christian Church in Ireland. There are two Methodist schools in the country: Methodist College Belfast in the North and Wesley College in the Republic. The Church is divided by geographical districts, with around 200 societies.

DID YOU KNOW?

Methodist President Eric Gallagher was the first Protestant churchman to meet with IRA leaders to try to end the Troubles in 1974.

PRESBYTERIAN CHURCH IN IRELAND

The first Presbytery was established in 1642 by Scottish Army members who were fighting in the Catholic Rebellion. Many Presbyterians emigrated to Ireland, particularly Ulster, from Scotland in the seventeenth century. The Church had a rocky start, as it faced opposition from Catholics and the established Anglican community. In 1840 a General Assembly united Covenanters (supporting parliamentarians against King Charles I) and Seceders (ruled by God alone, apolitical), and created the Presbyterian Church in Ireland. Today this is the largest Protestant denomination in the country.

QUAKER (SOCIETY OF FRIENDS)

The first meeting of the Society of Friends in Ireland took place in 1654 in Lurgan, County Armagh. Today there are 28 Meeting Houses throughout Ireland. In 2004 the Society held many festivities across the country to celebrate their 350th anniversary.

DID YOU KNOW?

'Quaker' is a nickname that started soon after the Society of Friends was established because they 'trembled at the word of the Lord', though it is now more common than the real name, even within the Society.

ROMAN CATHOLIC

The Catholic Church is the most populous Church in Ireland. Although numbers have reduced, 71 per cent of people on the island are still active members. Christianity arrived in Ireland in AD 461; though it was technically answerable to Rome, in practice the Church was a form of 'Celtic Christianity'. After the Normans conquered Ireland, the Church re-established itself there, creating the diocesan system that is still used today.

During the English Reformation, the Catholic religion became an important part of Irish identity. The Catholic Church had a strong influence over Irish society and this was exacerbated by the representatives of the Church being part of the early set-up of the Irish Free State and the 1937 Constitution stating that the Catholic Church had a 'special position' in Ireland. Although this is slowly changing, for a variety of reasons Ireland became a very conservative country: contraception was legalised in 1985, divorce became legal in 1996 and legislation for same-sex marriage followed in 2015 – but abortion remains illegal. The Church still has power within the school and health sectors, though there are many organisations trying to change this.

DID YOU KNOW?

Just under 97 per cent of Irish state primary schools are run by the Catholic Church.

SALVATION ARMY

The Salvation Army is run as an army (for people's souls), and the leader of the Church is called the General and based in England. The Salvation Army Ireland division refers to members in Northern Ireland and the Republic.

IRISH MYTHS AND FOLKLORE

Irish myths and legends have existed for thousands of years and throughout all those centuries they have been passed down through word of mouth. Storytelling was an important part of Irish society and poets held a high place on the social ladder. In Celtic society they spent many years learning their trade in special schools and were required to attain a high level of skill before they could be apprenticed to a poet. After a few years of apprenticeship they would qualify to travel throughout Ireland, reciting Irish myths and legends.

These myths and legends are still a large part of Irish society; they have influenced all aspects of the country's artistic history and continue to do so today. Most of the traditional ones, though not all, can be divided into four distinct cycles: Mythological Cycle, Ulster Cycle, Fenian Cycle and Historical Cycle. There are also folk tales that include the same characters, though those are not technically mythological. In the medieval era the stories were maintained by the monks, who began to write some of them down. However, as it was an oral tradition and the monks had to tell stories that could fit into a Christian framework – often deleting the Irish deities and reclassifying them as mortals – it is impossible to surmise how many of those tales and characters must have been lost in this time. Those that were recorded in monasteries make up the bulk of our knowledge today. Below is a little information on each of the four cycles and an example of a tale from each, as well as a list of Irish Celtic deities and characters.

MYTHOLOGICAL CYCLE

The Mythological Cycle focused on the Tuatha Dé Danann. These were the clan of gods (*tuath* being a word for 'tribe') that protected Ireland. As the monks weren't allowed to write about other deities, the gods became demoted to powerful humans rather than immortals. The Tuatha Dé Danann came from another world, accessible through the hills of Ireland called the Sidhe, which were all over the country (unlike in other cultures that had a single place, real or imagined, like Mount Olympus of Greek mythology or Asgard from Norse mythology), thus creating a close world filled with national and local gods. Like Norse gods, they were immortal but able to die: they would naturally last forever but could be killed as opposed to being immortal.

THE CHILDREN OF LIR (CLANN LIR)

When the Tuatha Dé Danann gathered to elect a new High King, it came down to a choice between two of the leaders: Bodb Derg and Lir. The former was elected to lead the Tuatha Dé Danann and the people of Ireland. Wanting to ensure that Lir would not oppose him, Bodb Derg gave him his daughter Aoibh. The pair were extremely happy and had four children: Fionnuala, Aodh and twins, Fiachra and Conn. Tragedy befell the family when Aoibh died. Bodb Derg sent Lir his other daughter, Aoife, who was not kind like her sister Aoibh and was jealous of the love that Lir had for his four children. Aoife decided she would have the children killed: she brought them out on a chariot one day to a lakeside and ordered her servant to kill them. The servant could not bring himself to raise the knife against them so Aoife, unable to murder her kin, used her dark magic to turn the four children into swans.

She sentenced them to live 300 years at Lough Derravaragh, 300 years in the Sea of Moyle and 300 years on the Isle of Inish Glora – in order to end the spell, they had to be blessed by a monk. When Bodb Derg found out what Aoife had done to his grandchildren, he turned her into an air demon and, stuck without a body, she was forced to travel the Earth for eternity. Fionnuala, Aodh, Fiachra and Conn all stayed on the lake and every day Lir would visit, and they would sing to him to console him.

Soon the news spread that four swans could sing with exceptional beauty so many people came to hear them. As time passed, Lir grew old and died, and the four swans were left with only each other for company, singing to the strangers who would gather by the lakeside. After 300 years on Lough

Derravaragh, the four children of Lir felt the lure of the spell calling them to the Sea of Moyle, between Ireland and Scotland. The Sea of Moyle was harsh and violent; it rose up in anger every season. For 300 years the four swans were tossed by waves and gales – throughout their struggles, they were often separated but they fought to stay together, always consoling each other and reminding themselves to have patience.

After another 300 years the swans were glad to feel the tug of the spell pulling them towards the Isle of Inish Glora in the western ocean. Inish Glora was cold and stormy: they froze in winter, slipping and sliding, and struggled to stay together. Finally, the day came when their 900-year banishment was over so they flew back to their father's old home only to find it abandoned and desolate. In sadness they returned to Inish Glora. One day they heard a bell; it was the first Christian bell in Ireland and the four swans were drawn to its peel. They went on land and at the church met Caomhog, who cared for them. Though rumours spread that these were the same mystical swans from 900 years before, few believed it was possible.

More and more people came to listen to them sing and one day the king of Connacht arrived, demanding ownership of the four swans. As Caomhog tried to explain that they were not his to offer, the king grew angry and tried to chain the swans together to steal them. A wind blew in from the sea, the bell began to toll, mist drifted in and the four swans were transformed back into children. The king ran away, frightened. The four children began to age very quickly so Caomhog hurriedly christened them before each one of them, now old, died and went to heaven.

ULSTER CYCLE
(OR RED BRANCH CYCLE)

The Ulster Cycle, unlike the other cycles, is concentrated in a geographical part of the island. Most of the action of the Ulster Cycle takes place in the provinces of Ulster and Connacht. During this time, Ireland didn't have a central authority but was a divided country with several kingdoms and *tuatha*. The stories focus on the reign of Conchobar Mac Nessa, king of Uslter. The most famous work from this cycle is the *Táin* (*Táin Bó Cúailnge*) – *The Cattle Raid of Cooley* – an epic story about a battle between Queen Maedhbh of Connacht and the Ulster men, as she attempted to steal a prize bull because of a tiff with her husband. Within the text are many short stories that pertain to the central plot: tales such as 'How Cú Chulainn Got His Name', 'Maedhbh and Ailill', 'Young Cú Chulainn', 'Deirdre of the Sorrows' and 'The Healing of Morrigan' are all contained within this text, though they are often told independently.

DID YOU KNOW?

Deirdre of the Sorrows was the last play that J. M. Synge worked on. He finished a draft but had not edited it. It is still performed, often unedited, to this day.

HOW CÚ CHULAINN GOT HIS NAME

Setanta was a young boy who lived with his mother, Deichtine, who was the sister of Conchobar Mac Nessa. His father was the god Lug. Setanta loved to hunt and play with his hurl and sliotar (hurling ball) but, as he lived in a secluded part of the country, he had a solitary upbringing. He begged his mother to bring him to his uncle in Emain Macha, which had one of the greatest armies in the kingdom and also a boys' troop where young boys were able to join and train to be great warriors. From the age of five Setanta wanted to attend but his mother complained that it was too far and explained that he would have to wait until he was older and could walk there himself. Setanta decided that he didn't want to wait – he took his toy spear, sliotar and hurl, and he set out on the road to Emain Macha. As he walked, he threw his sliotar into the sky, followed by his hurl so that it hit the sliotar further, and then his spear. Then he would run and try to catch each of them before they fell to the ground.

When Setanta reached Emain Macha, he saw the other boys playing hurling so he ran to join them, grabbing the ball and running with it. The boys were angry that he had not asked for their protection but Setanta, having never lived with anyone other than his mother and foster father, was not aware of the tradition. The boys ran over and attempted to beat Setanta who, filled with anger, began to hit each one of them so that they soon ran away. But Setanta pursued them, following them through Emain Macha.

Seeing a stranger chase his boy soldiers, Conchobar Mac Nessa grabbed Setanta and asked him who he was. Upon finding out that he had just come across his nephew, he explained the local custom to Setanta, who then asked for the boys' protection and was granted it. However, Setanta observed that they ought to ask him for *his* protection, since they had all run from him, and the boys agreed. After that he was admitted to the boys' troop of Emain Macha.

Conchobar watched with pride what a good warrior Setanta was growing up to be. One day he called out to Setanta as he was playing hurling and invited him to join at a king's meal that was being held for Conchobar at the house of Culann, his blacksmith. Setanta asked to be allowed to finish his game before he joined them for the dinner so Conchobar set off to the home of Culann. As the feast began, Culann asked if everyone was present and Conchobar, forgetting that Setanta had not yet arrived, said yes. Culann then set his fierce hound outside to guard them as they ate and drank.

Setanta ran through the forest, throwing his spear, hurl and sliotar up into the air as he made his way to Culann's home. When he arrived, the hound attacked and Setanta threw his sliotar with all his might into the jaws of the hound, choking the animal. Those inside heard the sounds of the fight and Conchobar remembered with fear that his little nephew was outside. Everyone stood still, worrying that the hound had killed the young boy but when they opened the door, they saw that Setanta was standing over the dead dog. Conchobar was delighted but Culann was furious: he was devastated that his best guard dog had been killed. He said that Setanta was welcome as an invitee of his uncle but not on his own. Setanta apologised for what he did, and promised to train a new hound and to act as a guard dog for Culann in the meantime. Conchobar laughed and said that all should call him *Cú Chulainn*, the hound of Culann, and that was how the great warrior, Cú Chulainn, got his name.

FENIAN CYCLE
(OR THE OSSIANIC CYCLE)

This cycle is narrated by the great bard Oisín, son of Fionn mac Cumhaill, and the stories are told mainly in verse. The cycle focuses on the escapades of the Fianna, an army that protected the whole of Ireland, led wisely by Demna, who was nicknamed Fionn because he was so fair. Two of the greatest Irish tales, *Tóraigheacht Dhiarmada agus Ghráinne (The Pursuit of Diarmaid and Gráinne)* and *Oisin in Tír na nÓg* form part of this cycle.

DID YOU KNOW?

The Diarmaid and Gráinne story, which is one of the few Fenian prose tales, is the Celtic source of *Tristan and Isolde.*

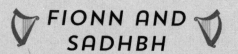

FIONN AND SADHBH

Fionn was out hunting in the woods when he came upon a doe grazing. He ordered his two hounds, Bran and Sceolan, to kill the animal but they wouldn't attack it so Fionn ran after the doe, which was extremely agile. Just as Fionn began to feel tired, he came upon his prey, who was sitting in the woods, with Bran and Sceolan resting with her. Fionn brought the doe back to his fort at Almú to protect the animal, knowing it must be magical.

That night Fionn awoke to find a beautiful woman in his chamber. She introduced herself as Sadhbh and explained to him that a spell had been put on her by Fear Dorcha that turned her into a deer. She had managed to escape him but had not been able to return herself to her human form – until she had stepped on Fionn's land. Fionn and Sadhbh fell in love and, as long as she stayed in Fionn's presence or on his land, their love was more powerful than the enchantment.

Fionn and Sadhbh were very happy together and soon she was pregnant. But Fionn had to go to war to protect the island, while Sadhbh remained at Almú and each day would climb the walls to look out for her love. One day she saw Fionn coming in the distance with Bran and Sceolan by his side. Sadhbh ran to meet him but the two hounds jumped and dragged her to their master who, with a flick of his cape, revealed himself to be Fear Dorcha. He took out his hazel wand and Sadhbh screamed as she was turned into a doe once more. The soldiers were horrified but in the time it took them to run to her aide, Fear Dorcha and Sadhbh were nowhere to be seen. They were powerless, as it had all happened so quickly.

When Fionn returned, he was devastated and went in search of Sadhbh. He travelled throughout Ireland for seven years, looking for his love. One day he came upon a little boy in the woods who had blond hair just like him and the eyes of Sadhbh. Bran and Sceolan ran to him and licked his face, nuzzling into him. The little boy was wild and couldn't speak but Fionn took him back to Almú. Once the boy learnt to talk, he explained that a deer had looked after him and fed him but she had been taken by Fear Dorcha. The little boy grew up to become a fine warrior and an exceptional poet. Fionn named him Oisín, meaning 'little fawn'.

HISTORICAL CYCLE (OR KINGS' CYCLES)

This cycle is a collection of Old and Middle Irish texts. The stories each revolve around Irish kings, though they are a combination of real monarchs in mythological stories with some mythological kings thrown into the mix. As the poets would record the genealogy of their patrons, the results were stories told by the bards to remember the great achievements of their patrons' families, as well as tales of great renown attributed to these dynasties. Nowadays, we are unsure whether Cormac mac Airt was a real person, though Brian Boru and Niall of the Nine Hostages most certainly had real-life counterparts.

BIRTH OF NIALL OF THE NINE HOSTAGES

King Eochaid Mugmedón was High King of Ireland and had five sons. The first four – Brian, Aillil, Fiachra and Fergus – were from his first wife, Mongfind, and the fifth was from a younger wife, a Saxon called Cairenn Chasdub that he had taken hostage. When Cairenn was pregnant, Mongfind put her to hard labour, hoping that she would miscarry. She beat her and treated her savagely. The entire household were extremely frightened of Mongfind, as she was a sorceress, so when they encountered Cairenn, they turned away. One day, as Cairenn was drawing water from a well, she went into labour. Fearing what Mongfind might to do her, she left her child by the well and returned with the water to the house. Everyone was too frightened of Mongfind to protect Cairenn or the child, so the baby was left beside the well.

He was found by an intelligent and kind poet, Torna, who named him Niall. When Torna picked the baby up, he had a vision and saw that Niall would grow to be an unopposed king of Ireland, and all of his descendants would be kings of Ireland. He raised Niall to be a thoughtful and understanding boy but, aware of his heritage and future, he also ensured that he received training to be a great warrior.

When Niall was of age, Torna took him to Tara, where the boy met his mother, who was still carrying buckets of water to and from the well. Niall ran to her, took the buckets and carried them to the house. Cairenn was overjoyed to meet her son, but she was still frightened of Mongfind. However, Niall told Cairenn not to worry and to dress well, for she too was a queen, and he brought her to sit on her throne, which had always been left empty. Mongfind was livid to see Cairenn sitting in the throne next to her own, but when Niall introduced himself, Eochaid was so delighted that he immediately called a celebration. Mongfind decided to bide her time and asked Eochaid to choose an heir to his throne. Unable to decide, he asked the Druid Sithchean to test them and discover which was best suited to the kingship. Sithchean told the five sons of Eochaid to go to the forge and make themselves a weapon but once they entered, he locked them in and set the place alight. The test was to see what they would save from the forge.

Brian came out first, carrying the hammers, which meant he would be strong in battles for the people. Fiachra carried out beer, which meant he would be popular. Aillil carried out the chest of weapons, which meant he would avenge the people. Fergus came out with a bundle of kindling, which meant he would be weak and would have no children. Niall came out from the forge carrying the anvil, meaning that he would be solid and the best king out of the five brothers.

Mongfind refused to accept this outcome. She told her sons to pretend to fight and kill Niall as if by accident when he intervened. So the four brothers went along with the plan and as Niall was about to try to calm them, Torna stopped him and advised that he leave Mongfind's children to sort out their quarrels themselves.

One day the five sons of Eochaid went hunting. They travelled far and ended up in an area that none of them knew. They caught some game and cooked it but had nothing to drink so became very thirsty. They sent Fergus to find some water. He searched without success for a long time and then came across a hideous hag guarding a well. She said that he could only have water if he gave her a kiss so he ran away back to his brothers, claiming that there was no water. Each of the brothers went in search of something to drink and each refused to kiss the crone, except Fiachra, who kissed her on the cheek. She told him that two of his descendants would become kings but wouldn't give him any water. At last Niall arrived and when the hag requested a kiss, he kissed her passionately and then took her in his arms to lie with her, and she was transformed into a beautiful woman. She told Niall that he would be king and that he should not give his brothers the water until they had sworn that they would never challenge his kingship.

Niall brought back the water and did as she had instructed. His brothers agreed and they returned to Tara. When they hung their weapons on the wall, Niall placed his on the top and when they sat to eat, he sat at the head of the table. When Mongfind and Eochaid asked them how their hunting had been, Niall answered. Mongfind corrected him, saying that Brian should speak, as he was the eldest, but her sons told her that they had given Niall dominion over them and he would be king.

Niall ruled for many years and had a peaceful reign. He conquered all of Ireland, England and Scotland, which totalled nine provinces. He took a hostage from each province to ensure that all of them would respect him. All of the kings of Ireland were descendant of Niall of the Nine Hostages.

DEITIES

It is difficult to be specific about the beliefs of the Irish Celtic and their gods, given the ulterior motives of those who recorded it. Nowadays, we are still unsure whether Irish gods had specific roles which have been lost to history or whether various localised gods have been interwoven into one. It is possible that many gods would have shared specific roles across different *tuatha* (the clans within the legends of these deities). They, like all Irish Celtic characters, have stories and histories rather than specific areas of spiritual expertise. Although it would be worth studying every one of them to see their histories, this would fill a book in its own right.

DID YOU KNOW?

Éire, the Irish word for Ireland, came from the goddess Ériu: one of three sisters who looked after Ireland. Banba and Fódla (the other two) have sometimes been used as the name for Ireland in older poetry.

TUATHA DÉ DANANN

Tuatha Dé Danann defeated the Fomorians and were then defeated by the Milesians. The Irish Celtic gods (like most gods) mirrored the culture they were revered by, with gods having skirmishes and changing alliances.

Dagda – High King of the Tuatha Dé Danann. He had a magic club that could kill nine men with one blow but the handle could bring a man back to life. He also had a cauldron that never emptied so no person went hungry.

Danu – Mother of the Tuatha Dé Danann. Danann is a reference to Danu and it means 'the tribe of Danu'.

Óengus – Dagda's son; he had singing birds circling his head.

Bodb Derg – The son of Dagda and the king of Munster, he was voted king of Tuatha Dé Danann.

Lug – A young warrior and saviour, Lug has often been compared to Christ in early Christian writings. He was the son of Dagda, father of Setanta, and came to save Cú Chulainn in his final battle. Often depicted with birds flying around his head, he was said to be good at all arts, truth and law. He is also the namesake of Lughnasadh, the harvest festival and the root for *Lúnasa*, which is the Irish for the month of August.

Morrígan – One of three sisters: Badb, Macha and Morrígan. War goddesses with the ability to change shape, it was good to have them on your side, as they tended to kill or seriously harm anyone who crossed them.

Lir – God of the sea (unsurprisingly, father of the children of Lir).

Dian Cecht – God of healing.

Brigid – Goddess of poets and spring. Brigid is said to have two sisters, Brigid the Healer and Brigid the Smith. Some argue they were all one, whereas others claim that local goddesses had the same name, causing confusion later. The Christian St Brigid's feast day is the same as the pagan festival that celebrated Brigid, on the first day of spring.

Etaín – Goddess of the sun, she has an epic tale of her own, which is well worth a read: *Tochmarc Étaíne* or *The Wooing of Étaín*.

Clíodhna – Queen of the banshees.

Áine – Goddess of love, wealth and summer.

Banba, Ériu and Fódla – Triumvirate of goddesses who protected Ireland.

Manannán mac Lir – Son of Lir (it can also mean son of the sea). There is no consensus on whether he was a son from another marriage of Lir or a different god of the sea. He married Fann, the queen of the otherworld, and is said to be the ferryman between both worlds.

Ogma – A warrior and prize fighter for Nuadu Airgetlám (first king of Tuatha Dé Danann); the creator of Ogham.

Trí Dé Dana – Smiths of the Tuatha Dé Danann. **Credne** was the metal worker, **Goibniu** the axe maker and **Luchtaine** the carpenter. They made all of the weapons that the Tuatha Dé Danann used to fight the Fomorians.

FOMORIANS

The Fomorians were villainous creatures, often depicted as giants and monsters, which were the first inhabitants of Ireland. They fought the Tuatha Dé Danann and all but one were killed, though they return throughout the legends, causing trouble and generally being baddies.

Balor – He could destroy people just by looking at them with his front eye (he had one eye on his forehead and one on his back). During battle Lug pulled it out and used it to kill the other Fomorians.

Buarainech – Balor's father.

Cethlenn – Balor's wife and Ethniu's mother. Cethlenn was a seer who warned Balor that he would be killed by his grandson.

Cíocal Gricenchos – First leader of the Fomorians.

Elatha – King of the Fomorians. His son Bres (from Ériu) was king of Tuatha Dé Danann but preferred his Fomorian heritage and enslaved the Tuatha Dé Danann, until they revolted and killed him.

Tethra – The ruler of Mag Mell (a paradise that you can only enter if you had a noble death – a heroes-only heaven, if you will), similar to Valhalla in Norse mythology.

Ethniu – Daughter of Balor and Cethlann. After her mother's prophesy, Ethniu was trapped in a tower but Cían broke in and she had triplets. Balor ordered them to be killed but one was dropped in the harbour and grew up to be Lug, who, as predicted by Cethlenn, killed his grandfather.

MILESIANS

The Milesians were the final gods to rule Ireland. They came from Iberia and defeated the Tuatha Dé Danann.

Amergin Glúingel – *Filid* (a combination of a poet and judge) of the Milesians.

Eber Finn – Son of Míl Espáine and king of Ireland.

Érimón Finn – Son of Míl Espáine and king of Ireland

Míl Espáine – King of Spain who travelled to Ireland because it was prophesised that his sons would rule the country. He died but his wife, Scota, brought their eight sons to Ireland. The Tuatha Dé Danann caused a tempest to stop them, killing most of her children, but ultimately the Milesians took over from the Tuatha Dé Danann to be in control of Ireland.

FOLKLORE

Ireland is filled with folklore (the term was coined in the 1800s when writers began to collect the local stories and record them). Many of the characters are reoccurring, often living in another realm but visiting Ireland. The stories pertain to a land full of mischief, magic and wisdom. Great use is made of this version of Ireland by the tourist industry, though many of the superstitions still exist. Undoubtedly, the Irish still enjoy folklore, which is passed on to children by parents and within schools, even if not really believed anymore.

Every corner of the island has local folklore and legends that are specific to the area. Many place names derive from local legends; for example, the Boyne Valley and river take their name from the goddess Boand. Nowadays, the most famous character is the leprechaun, but there are many other mythical creatures that litter our folklore. Below is a taste of some of them you should look out for or avoid. Most of the folklore contains characters that come from the Sídhe, the same land of the hills where the gods came from.

SHEE

For want of a better term, this is often translated as 'fairies', though in reality the word referred to myriad different spirits and beings with magical qualities. The Sídhe were the mythical entrances or worlds within the hills and Aes Sídhe the people that hailed from this place. These were gods, fairies and several other creatures. The name was anglicised to Shee and at some point became 'the little people', though there is nothing to suggest that the Aes Sídhe were diminutive as the leprechaun was.

LEPRECHAUN

A small cobbler (nowadays dressed in green) with a leather pinny (apron), carrying a hammer and protecting a pot of gold at the end of a rainbow. They are said to be quick both in wit and movement, and if you catch one, you should never take your eyes off him even for a moment because he will disappear.

CLURICAUN

Sometimes considered the same as a leprechaun or related to one, this small being is always drunk and a little bit mean (a leprechaun on a bad day). They are thieves and tricksters, and sometimes take a joyride on dogs and sheep. They like to cause mayhem but not in the fun, cheeky ways of other Sídhe.

FEAR DEARG

Often written 'Far Derrig', as the anglicised pronunciation which translates as 'red man'. Some say that they are the same as leprechauns, while others believe that the two are closely related. The name implies that he wears red, though apparently the colour may also come from his bloody deeds. He is a grisly practical joker and often believed to be the one who placed the changelings.

CHANGELINGS

These were fairies that looked like children but enjoyed misery befalling the family. They were usually believed to be switched at birth, though a sudden change in demeanour was a signifier that your child had been taken by the fairies (I can't help but feel the issue must have been pandemic with toddlers). It was said that if the mother crossed a river with the changeling in her arms, the child would be returned. Also, there was a possibility of luring out the changeling with music.

FAIRY BUSH

I imagine this is probably no longer relevant, but it was said that when there is a bush in the centre of a field, the farmer should never chop it or his whole family will have bad luck. This is because the fairies would dance around the bush at night.

PÚCA (PRONOUNCED 'POOKA')

Also called phuca, poc and ghor, these mischievous sprites came into your home and caused trouble – both on a small and large scale, for instance turning milk sour or stealing your baby. They often took the form of a goat (the Irish word for goat is *poc*) and they also had a penchant for causing maritime incidents.

DID YOU KNOW?

The character of Puck from Shakespeare's *A Midsummer Night's Dream* is said to be named after the mythical púca.

BANSHEE

The literal translation of this is 'woman spirit'. To hear the banshee's scream was foretelling the death of someone close to you and anyone who saw a banshee would die on the spot. Despite this, there are various descriptions: mostly depicting an old woman in rags, though sometimes her antithesis – a young beautiful woman.

ABHARTACH

Pronounced 'a-var-tock', this was a dwarf-like creature from a small area called Slaughtaverty, Co. Derry. The creature, which was causing havoc amongst the local tribe, was killed and buried by the chief. It then returned and began to drink the blood of the tribe. The chief caught and killed the Abhartach again, burying him standing up, but it returned once more and continued to drink the blood of the tribe. Finally, the chief asked a Druid what to do, and his advice was to kill the Abhartach with a wooden sword and bury him upside-down, placing a large stone on top. The Abhartach was caught and buried as the Druid advised. Although the Abhartach could not be killed, as he was *neamh-mharbh* – neither dead nor alive – he could be stopped. Rumours still circulate about horrible things that happen in this area and the stone laid on the Abhartach's grave can still be visited.

DID YOU KNOW?

The Abhartach is credited as one of the inspirations of Dublin-born writer Bram Stoker in creating his character, Dracula.

FEAR GORTA

Translated as 'the hungry man', he is a spirit that takes the form of a starving corpse and roams the country, asking for aid. He brings good luck to any who help him. On the flipside, he will curse any who don't help him to live out their lives in misery, poverty and hunger without any reprieve.

FEAR DORCHA

Pronounced 'far dur-ka', the name translates as 'the dark man'. He is an evil spirit that is sometimes said to work for the queen of the otherworld. A cruel tyrant who captures mortals, he is the most evil of the Irish folklore characters and was substituted for the devil in some later stories in Christian times.

SLUAGH
Pronounced 'sloo-ah', this translates as 'group' and refers to a mob of the restless dead. They would fly through the air and try to break into the homes of the recently departed to take the soul of the dead person with them.

ELLÉN TRECHEND
A three-headed monster for whom there is very little information – definitely not one of the good creatures, though.

MERROWS
From the Irish *murúch*, these are merpeople. They are both male and female in Irish folklore, and they wear a *cohuleen druith* – a type of hat that enables them to breathe underwater. If they lose it, they are trapped on land. They are kind, sweet and good. In some tales they marry humans, though when these marriages happen, the merrow is treated badly by their spouse (often having their *cohuleen druith* stolen) and they eventually return to the sea.

SELCHIES
These are creatures who live as seals in water but can shed that skin and transform into humans on land. They then need their skins to be able to return to the water. They spend their lives desiring what they don't have, always wishing to be in the water when they're on land and vice versa.

PORTRAIT OF A PROVINCE: CONNACHT

Connacht is the western province of Ireland, originally consisting of the independent kingdoms Iarthar Connacht, Lúighne and Uí Maine. It is named after the ruling tribe 'Connachta', descendants of the mythical King Conn of the Hundred Battles. Despite being colonised by the English, their constant attacks meant that the invading force struggled to control this region and the colonists who survived largely became Gaelicised. Connacht has the highest number of Irish speakers of any of the provinces in the country – there are over 40,000. It was hit harder than any other province by the Great Famine in the 1840s and lost over 400,000 people to emigration and death. Today ghost villages can still be visited, where empty cottages are all that remain after the inhabitants packed up their belongings and emigrated as a group to start new lives abroad.

GALWAY – GAILLIMH

Nickname: The Tribesmen

Song: 'Fields of Athenry', 'Galway Bay'

The name of Galway originates from the Irish name for the river (now named the Corrib). Galway is both the name of the county and the capital city. The nickname 'city of the tribes' comes from the merchants (Gaelicised Normans) who ran the area. Galway was a major trading hub in the Middle Ages, particularly with France and Spain. Nowadays, the city is famous for its culture scene, with several festivals taking place every year and a thriving arts community. It is also home to the National University of Ireland, Galway, which was established in 1845, and is known for its arts courses and the marine sciences.

DID YOU KNOW?

Galway is home to Connemara, the largest Gaeltacht (Irish-speaking) region in Ireland (and, presumably, the world).

LEITRIM – LIATROIM

Nickname: Wild Rose County

Song: 'Lovely Leitrim'

Leitrim means 'grey ridge' and is named after a village within the county. Partly due to the number of bogs and lakes and the mountainous terrain, it is the least populated of any county in Ireland. Leitrim was part of the Kingdom of Breifne, though it has always remained quite insular. It was hit by a recession in the 1830s brought on by the mechanisation of linen weaving and later, in the next decade, it suffered greatly in the Great Famine, when a continuous stream of emigration began and continued until the twenty-first century. Today Leitrim has the fastest growing population in Connacht.

DID YOU KNOW?

Seán Mac Diarmada, one of the leaders of the Easter Rising in 1916, was from Leitrim. He was executed at Kilmainham Gaol.

MAYO – MAIGH EO

Nickname: The Westerners

Song: 'Moonlight on Mayo'

County Mayo translates as 'plain of the yew trees' and is a mix of bog, limestone and subsoil named after a village within the county. Achill Island – Ireland's largest island – lies off the coast of Mayo. Thanks to the bogs, there is a wealth of well-preserved archaeological history, which has provided excellent artefacts from the Mesolithic and Neolithic Stone Age, as well as the Bronze and Iron Ages. The county also has several examples of megalithic tombs.

DID YOU KNOW?

Mayo is home to Ireland's only fjord, which is at Killary Harbour, at the foot of Mweelrea.

FAMOUS FIGURES
GRÁINNE MHAOL (c.1530–1603)

Gráinne Mhaol was a pirate and chieftain in Mayo in the late 1500s and early 1600s. Legend tells us that the young Gráinne wanted to go to sea with her father and, for that reason, she cut off her hair and dressed as a boy. She was recognised by her father's crew and nicknamed Gráinne Mhaol (*mhaol* being the Irish word for 'bald'), but nevertheless went off to sea. When Gráinne divorced her first husband, she kept their lands, and later, upon his death, she inherited her father's fleet and his business ('business' being a generous term for piracy).

As a wealthy landowner, when her sons were taken captive and incarcerated by the governor of Connacht, she personally requested an audience with Queen Elizabeth I. During this meeting, despite the fact that Gráinne refused to bow before her and was found to be carrying a dagger, Queen Elizabeth ignored her courtiers' objections and accepted that Gráinne had not meant any harm. After the meeting, Gráinne Mhaol agreed to stop supporting the Irish rebellion and Elizabeth agreed to remove Sir Bingham from his position of power, therefore allowing Gráinne's sons to be freed. After a few years Sir Bingham was returned to power by the queen and Gráinne Mhaol resumed her support of the Irish revolutionaries.

DID YOU KNOW?

Queen Elizabeth I and Gráinne Mhaol conducted their meeting in Latin, as neither spoke the other's native tongue.

ROSCOMMON – ROS COMÁN

Nickname: The Sheepstealers

Song: 'Man of Roscommon'

Roscommon means 'the woods of Comán' (Comán was an abbot who founded a monastery in AD 550). The river Shannon to the east and the river Suck in the southwest frame the county. There are several islands in Roscommon, including 32 of them in lake Lough Key. Rath Cruachán, a complex of archaeological sites, was the seat of Queen Meadhbh, the real-life version of the legendary queen of Connacht. Boyle, in Roscommon, is the setting for the television series *Moone Boy*, loosely based on the childhood of the comedian Chris O'Dowd.

DID YOU KNOW?

Roscommon boasts the longest life expectancy in Ireland (75.6 years for men and 82.4 for women).

DID YOU KNOW?

Carnagh East is the geographical centre of Ireland.

SLIGO - SLIGEACH

Nickname: Yeats' men

Song: 'The Isle of Innisfree' or 'Down by the Sally Gardens'

Sligo means 'place of shells' and it was originally the name of the river Garavogue. Sligo has many prehistoric archaeological sites and is the only town in which all classes of Irish megalithic monuments are found. The first farms were excavated in Sligo and many believe that the Cuil Irra Peninsula is the tomb of Queen Meadhbh, who reigned over Connacht around the third century and was the real-life incarnation of the fierce warrior queen found in Irish mythology.

DID YOU KNOW?

John Yeats spent his summers in Sligo, raising his children. Sligo influenced their work – most famously, the poetry of William Butler and Jack's paintings.

LAKE ISLE OF INNISFREE

I will arise and go now, and go to Innisfree,
And a small cabin build there,
of clay and wattles made;
Nine bean rows will I have there,
a hive for the honey bee,
And live alone in the bee loud glade.

And I shall have some peace there,
for peace comes dropping slow,
Dropping from the veils of the morning
to where the cricket sings;
There midnight's all a glimmer,
and noon a purple glow,
And evening full of the linnet's wings.

I will arise and go now, for always night and day
I hear lake water lapping with low sounds by the shore;
While I stand on the roadway,
or on the pavements grey,
I hear it in the deep heart's core.

W. B. YEATS

THE ARTS

LITERATURE

'Ireland is a nation of poets/writers/storytellers' is about the most common phrase I've come across while researching this book. Apart from those highflyers – Italy and Greece – we have the oldest literary tradition in Europe. Ireland has a strong heritage of ground-breaking and form-changing writers, as well as writers whose work captured the nation or specific eras in history, such as Bram Stoker, James Joyce, W. B. Yeats, Colm Toibin, Roddy Doyle and Louise O'Neill.

FAMOUS FIGURES
MARIA EDGEWORTH (1767–1849)

Novels began to become popular in Ireland in the early nineteenth century. One of the first writers to find success was Maria Edgeworth with her book *Castle Rackrent* (1800). This was the first novel to address the Ascendancy landlords and it started a long history of books based on the 'big house'. Maria was the daughter of Richard Lovell Edgeworth, an unusual Anglo-Irish landlord who, ignoring the Penal Laws, would grant security to tenants. He raised his children to follow the philosophy of Jean Jacques Rousseau – to seek, explore and enjoy education. Maria's first book was published in 1795. During the 1798 Rebellion, Maria's family had to flee their house for safety but their fair treatment of their tenants meant that when they returned, they found that only a few windows had been broken. With the success of her writings, she grew in notoriety. Jane Austen and John Ruskin were admirers of her work, as were William Wordsworth, Lord Byron and Sir Walter Scott, who all visited her at Edgeworth. She retired to run the estate upon the death of her father. While her brother squandered their inheritance, she was able to sustain the estate from her literary earnings. She worked throughout the Famine, distributing food, and soliciting her friends and admirers for funds. In 1848 she came out of retirement with a children's story to raise money for famine relief.

DID YOU KNOW?

Jonathan Swift was the Dean of St Patrick's Cathedral, Dublin. He is most famous for his book *Gulliver's Travels*.

IRISH LITERARY RENAISSANCE

In the late nineteenth and early twentieth centuries, Irish writers focused on celebrating Irish heritage. The movement worked in tandem with the political direction towards nationalism. The majority of writers who belonged to this movement were from the Anglo-Irish community. They glorified what they perceived as the simplicity and natural beauty of the Irish peasants, considering them the 'true Irish'.

FAMOUS FIGURES
W. B. YEATS (1865-1939)

One of the leaders of the Irish Literary Renaissance was William Butler Yeats. He was born in Dublin, and although he moved to London at a young age, he spent much of his childhood with his maternal grandparents in Sligo. When he was a teenager, he returned with his parents to Dublin where he attended Dublin's Metropolitan School of Art in 1883, which introduced him to fellow artists. He was a talented poet, though he also collected Irish folklore with Lady Gregory and wrote essays on the importance of the arts over politics. He began the Irish Literary Theatre, and wrote and directed plays, as well as aiding the running of the theatre. In 1922, he accepted the Irish Free State's invitation to become a senator, serving for six years. In 1923 he was awarded the Nobel Prize for Literature.

DID YOU KNOW?

Despite Ireland's history of great writers, books in Ireland were heavily censored. Censorship in the Irish Free State was extremely strict, influenced by Catholic morality. The original committee set up to tackle this was given the dramatic title 'The Committee on Evil Literature', though it was later rebranded as the Censorship of Publications Board. The board is still active today and banned *The Raped Little Runaway* by Jean Martin in 2016. Prior to this, the most recently banned book was in 1998. The censorship law limited the censorship to 12 years, though it could be renewed.

FAMOUS FIGURES
JAMES JOYCE (1882-1941)

James Joyce was born in Dublin and is one of the most celebrated writers in the history of English literature. He is revered in Ireland, though he personally found the country socially too oppressive. He travelled throughout the Continent and rarely returned to Ireland after 1904. His greatest work is *Ulysses*, which is an early example of stream of consciousness being used as a narrative device. The story takes place over the course of one day, from the internal monologue of Leopold Bloom. Despite no longer living in Ireland, the majority of his work – including *Dubliners*, *Finnegans Wake* and *A Portrait of the Artist as a Young Man* – is set there.

FAMOUS FIGURES
PATRICK KAVANAGH (1904-1967)

Patrick Kavanagh was the first poet to record modern agricultural life in his contemporary Ireland. He left school at 12 to apprentice as a cobbler but, lacking natural aptitude, he left and spent the next 15 years helping on his family's farm. He began writing poems during this time and his first piece was published in a local paper in 1928. Kavanagh hated the romanticised version of country life written by the Celtic revivalists and wrote in opposition to that. He was disliked by his contemporaries, as they were all members of the Anglo-Irish elite, and he was often referred to as 'that Monaghan boy'. In 1954 he was diagnosed with cancer and had a lung removed. After this ordeal, he was filled with a joy for life and created some of his best work, finally receiving acclaim. In April 1967 he married Katharine Maloney but died later that year.

FAMOUS FIGURES
SEAMUS HEANEY (1939–2013)

Seamus Heaney was born in County Derry, the eldest of nine children. He won a scholarship to a boarding school in the city of Derry and later moved to Belfast during the early years of the Troubles. Heaney was influenced by his father's agricultural background, the industrial history of his mother's family and the political conflict that surrounded him in Northern Ireland. His poetry is considered some of the best work of the twentieth century and in 1995 he was awarded the Nobel Prize for Literature. He also wrote plays and translated from several languages, most famously *Beowulf* from Old English. He taught at Harvard University and served as an Oxford professor.

DID YOU KNOW?

Dublin is the only city in the world to have produced three winners of the Nobel Prize for Literature.

FAMOUS FIGURES
LOUISE O'NEILL (1985–)

Louise O'Neill is a feminist writer of books for young adults (YA) as well as non-YA. She was born in west Cork, where she still lives today. She has won several awards for her debut novel *Only Ever Yours* and also for *Asking For It*. Her books explore gritty subject matters with considerable agility. Her first book was re-released with an adult cover due to its popularity. She also writes a column for the *Irish Examiner*, with candid honesty, about her experiences of sex, feminism and life in general.

IRISH LANGUAGE LITERATURE

In the late sixteenth century the role of the *filí* (travelling poets) was waning, as they were distrusted by the British elite. As musicians were still used, the two roles merged and lyrics began to be put to music. The musicians used the old works of the poets and this practice, which continued into the eighteenth century, ensured the survival of traditional Irish poetry. The eighteenth century saw the rise of *aislingí*, a form of nationalist poetry where the poet has a vision of a beautiful woman who declares herself to be Ireland and bemoans her oppression. However, as English language was becoming popular and fewer people were reading Irish works, they went out of fashion.

Irish language literature was almost completely forgotten until the Gaelic revival in the late nineteenth century when the Old and Middle Irish texts were rediscovered and translated. Padraig Pearse wrote poetry, short stories and plays in Irish. His most famous work is *Mise Eire*. Douglas Hyde (first president of Ireland) became an activist in 'de-anglicising Ireland'. He wrote newspaper articles and journals in Irish, and his plays were performed at the Abbey.

In the twentieth century Irish language literature was greatly reduced. Autobiographies became popular in the early twentieth century; three of them came from the now uninhabited Blasket Islands – *Peig Sayers, Muiris ÓSuilleabhain* and *Tomás Ó Criomhthain* – and their English translations remain popular. Today short stories and poetry in Irish are more common than novels but all are in little demand.

MUSIC

Ireland has added a whole host of names to the international stage, such as U2, Van Morrison and Sinéad O'Connor to name but a few. The Irish have produced various genres but are undoubtedly known for their traditional music which, unlike many other types of folk music from around the world, continues to be played informally and to popular demand. Many pubs all over the country invite musicians to play as a means of bringing in tourists. To this day, you can still happen upon a 'session' in a pub, particularly in the west of Ireland. Sessions – traditionally in homes, though now almost always in a pub – are informal groups playing music together. The players join and leave freely as the music continues, often stepping out to chat, drink or have a smoke. Although locals will actively try to avoid the tourist traps of an organised group of musicians, an impromptu session is generally very popular with all age groups who come in to enjoy the music and the atmosphere. The Willy Clancy Summer School, which is held over a week each August in Miltown Malbay, Co. Clare, is a particularly good example.

Traditional music is still passed down from generation to generation and taught by ear, though it is now widely available as sheet music. Although most traditional forms went out of fashion with the coming of the industrial age, it remained popular long after other countries had moved on and in the early part of the twentieth century it regained popularity, as people began to focus on the differences between Ireland and England. Its success waned slightly in the mid-twentieth century but in the 1960s, thanks to the rise of all folk music, it experienced a resurgence. It was during this time that Seán Ó Riada began his work on Irish music and Francis O'Neill started collecting Irish works.

Most Irish folk music is paired with dance styles (jigs, reels, polkas, etc.), though slow airs (a misleading title, as few are simply slow) focus on storytelling. These are created with storytelling in mind through the tune of the music, which lilts fast and slow, taking the audience on a journey. Often they don't have a chorus, as there is no need for repetition in such a piece – a good example of this is *The Fox Chase*. Slow airs can be performed on any instrument but they are most popular sung in the Sean Nós style (a highly ornamented unaccompanied style without metronomic rhythm) and on the uilleann pipes; they can also be thoroughly impressive on a tin whistle if you're lucky enough to find a gifted player.

FAMOUS FIGURES
TURLOUGH O'CAROLAN (1670–1738)

Turlough O'Carolan was an Irish composer and harpist from Co. Meath. He was educated by his father's employers (his father was a blacksmith) and was a skilled poet. He was blinded in 1688 by smallpox and then apprenticed to a harper to learn the trade. O'Carolan was a traditional harpist who was influenced by European classical music. In 1691, at the age of 21, he began to travel throughout Ireland, composing songs for patrons. He continued to do this for over 50 years. He sang only in Irish and is believed to have had limited English (only one of his compositions was written in English). Today his music is more commonly performed in English, having been posthumously written and translated, though some works were printed during his lifetime. He is believed to have coined the term 'planxty': an upbeat song written in celebration of a cheerful and generous patron.

FAMOUS FIGURES
FRANCIS O'NEILL (1848–1936)

We know much of the Irish music thanks to Francis O'Neill, both for his tireless work collecting it and for the part he played in creating an interest. O'Neill was born in Co. Cork but moved to America when he was very young, growing up to be the chief of police in Chicago, Illinois. He was a talented fiddler, piper and flautist, and a prominent member of the sizable Irish immigrant population in Chicago. This community held on fiercely to their identity and as Ireland began to lose some of its interest in its musical heritage, the various immigrant groups across the world became a valuable source of traditional Irish music. O'Neill enjoyed collecting Irish music, asking musicians to write down their pieces and send them to him. Upon retiring, he began to publish the thousands of songs he had collected.

FAMOUS FIGURES
SEÁN Ó RIADA (1931–1971)

Seán Ó Riada was born in Cork in 1931. He was extremely influential in the revival of Irish music, as a composer, conductor, music director and producer. He played the violin, organ, piano, harpsichord, clarsach and bodhrán (see p.191). He played with dance bands throughout his youth, and later he worked for the radio and as the music director for the Abbey Theatre. He composed many pieces for both of these institutions. Though Irish traditional music had remained popular amongst immigrant communities in Britain and North America, it had nearly died out in Ireland. Seán Ó Riada created a group, Ceoltóirí Chualann, who dressed like a showband but performed as a traditional group. This gifted man was also appointed Professor of Music at University College Cork.

FAMOUS FIGURES
THE CLANCY BROTHERS

The Clancy Brothers and Tommy Makem rose to fame in the US as part of the American folk music revival in the 1960s and 1970s. The group originally consisted of three of the Clancy brothers from Carrick-on-Suir, Co. Tipperary, and their friend Tommy Makem from Keady, Co. Armagh. They played various instruments and sang traditional songs, though they often turned ballads into upbeat numbers, much to the chagrin of some traditionalists. The group had many incarnations, with all four of the Clancy brothers mixing and matching, as well as two of their sons/nephews. At the height of their fame they each wore an Aran sweater while on a TV show (a present from the Clancys' mum because she'd read it would be a hard winter), which led to a huge rise in the jumper's sales and the group having a 'look'. The group found fame in the US and when an Irish radio presenter came across them while on holiday, he brought their works back to Ireland. They soon achieved international fame and led the revival of traditional Irish music in Ireland, as well as further afield.

DID YOU KNOW?

Bob Dylan cites The Clancy Brothers as one of his early and most important inspirations. They worked together and were friends in the Greenwich Village music scene of 1960s New York.

Sharon Shannon is a famous traditional musician best known for her accordion work, though she also plays the fiddle, tin whistle and melodeon. She began playing at a young age and had her first tour of the US with Disirt Tola when she was 14. In the late 1980s she joined the Waterboys. She released her first album, *Sharon Shannon*, in 1991, which is still the best-selling traditional Irish music album in Ireland. She remains one of the most popular traditional Irish musicians in the country today.

INSTRUMENTS

There are many instruments that are associated with traditional Irish music. The fiddle is synonymous with it, yet the instrument is and always was the classical violin, designed by the Italians in the baroque era. Referring to it as a fiddle is referencing the music that will be played rather than the instrument. Other instruments, such as the accordion, melodeon and concertina, are common in Irish music, though they too were imported, long after the traditional Irish music style had been established. These foreign instruments suited the music, especially their agility in mastering upbeat tempos. Their place on the Irish music scene was solidified in the 1960s folk music resurgence and this period also introduced some instruments that have now become staples in the Irish scene, such as the mandolin, guitar, banjo and the bouzouki. The following sections describe traditional instruments that have been used in Ireland for centuries.

Uilleann Pipes

The uilleann pipes are a type of bagpipe particular to Ireland. They are considered one of the most difficult instruments to learn, and they have more of a range than other bagpipes and a lighter sound. Most bagpipes were war instruments but there is no evidence of the uilleann pipes being used for this purpose.

Tin Whistle
This traditional woodwind instrument has similar counterparts across the world. The whistle comes in various keys, though the most popular is a D whistle. It is commonly taught in schools, often acting as an introduction to music for many Irish children.

Irish Flute
It is played like a classical flute, but it is made of wood. Some Irish flutes simply have holes, though they now generally have keys, like their metal counterparts. Although the Irish flute is a popular traditional instrument in Ireland, it is not native to the island, having been inspired by the Western concert flute.

Bodhrán
The bodhrán is a hand-held drum, with a single round frame made of wood and a thin goatskin nailed across one side. The player tunes the drum with their hand as they play. There is a single drumstick called a 'tipper', which is held in the middle; both ends of the tipper are used to beat the drum.

Harp
There are many forms of harp across the world, but the harp traditionally used in Irish music is the 'Celtic harp', sometimes called a *cláirseach*, from its original Irish form. It is smaller than classical harps – traditionally strung with brass wires, the chamber is carved from a single willow log.

DID YOU KNOW?

Ireland is the only country that has a musical instrument as its national emblem.

DID YOU KNOW?

The harp used as a state symbol for Ireland is based on the Trinity College harp (sometimes known as 'Brian Boru Harp') and is possibly the oldest harp in the world. It is on display at Trinity College, Dublin.

THEATRE

FROM THE FIFTEENTH TO THE EIGHTEENTH CENTURY

Theatre was introduced to Ireland by the British. Prior to this, performance, storytelling and music were an important part of Irish culture. There were also liturgical performances in Ireland, but theatre as we know it, and as Ireland is now famous for, was a British form of entertainment. In 1601, as Hugh O'Neill was in the middle of his revolution, Lord Mountjoy had the play *Gorboduc* performed as part of the Christmas festivities at Dublin Castle. *Gorboduc* was a British play (it served as Shakespeare's primary influence for *King Lear*) and, notably, focused on the danger of splitting a territory.

By 1637, Ireland had its first theatre and theatre group, including a resident playwright. 'His Majesty's Company of Comedians' comprised quite a prestigious group of actors, primarily because London theatres had been closed due to the plague in 1636, giving the new Irish theatre group their choice of the best performers. In the 1640s the administration and its theatre decanted to Kilkenny. However, by the 1660s, Dublin was once again the centre of action and the new style of theatre, complete with proscenium arch, was built at Smock Alley (its shell still exists). This theatre was home to John Ogilby, the king's appointed 'Master of Revels in Ireland'.

Throughout the 1700s theatre gained popularity all around Ireland and soon plays by Irish writers and performers were being staged. These works were highly contentious and theatres were stuck between two polar opposites of political and religious belief. Pastorals and comedies became the most common (and safest) choice but by the time the fight for emancipation was in full swing in the early nineteenth century, this balance became impossible. Theatre audiences, often divided by wealth, were also divided by their views on Catholic emancipation. The theatres began to be split by interest and the content of their plays. Despite this divide in Irish theatres, two of the most successful British writers of this era – Oliver Goldsmith and Richard Brinsley Sheridan – were both Irish, though based in London.

DID YOU KNOW?

Smock Alley Theatre is the oldest theatre in Dublin, having opened its doors in 1662 (it is never referred to as Ireland's oldest theatre and yet, I can find no examples of an older one in the country). The once lavish interiors were stripped out in the late eighteenth century when it became a warehouse and then later a church, until 2012, when it was restored back to its original role as a theatre.

THE NINETEENTH CENTURY

Although around this time the music hall was the most popular place for entertainment in Ireland, some great works of drama and comedy in traditional theatres were also very popular. Nineteenth-century theatre was full of wit and three writers stood out on the London stage, famed for their skill in clever wordplay. Oscar Wilde, George Bernard Shaw and Dion Boucicault were from Dublin and, though contemporaries, tackled the industry in very different ways. Wilde considered life an enactment of art. Boucicault, on the other hand, preferred to make money rather than poetry, and Shaw was an active socialist who buried philosophical and political questions within his sharp lines.

FAMOUS FIGURES
DION BOUCICAULT (c.1820–1890)

Dion Boucicault became one of the most successful playwrights in the English-speaking world, within his lifetime. He lived in

London for ten years, moved to America, where he became an extremely popular and famous playwright, and then returned to Ireland with his US and London success, *The Octoroon*, about slavery in America. Boucicault's play was popular with both sides of the emancipation arguments. It was not contentious because it was a foreign issue, it was a love story and it had a happy ending (changed from the sad one in America) – also, it was already a huge success. The play – seen by Queen Victoria in London three times – had sold out in the US and was hailed as an Irish success because of the home-grown writer.

Boucicault wrote popular comedies but his Irish characters, usually played by himself, were loveable, wily and courageous. They went against the stereotypical portrayal of the Irish drunk but were familiar enough not to lose the English and American audiences. He was primarily interested in making money, something he openly admitted, which led to him adapting his plays so they would seem local and thus entice a bigger crowd. The best example of this is his play *The Poor of New York*, which he reworked multiple times to create: *The Poor of Leeds*, *The Poor of Manchester*, *The Streets of Dublin*, and so on.

IRISH LITERARY REVIVAL ON STAGE

The nineteenth century also saw the beginning of the Irish Literary Revival that promoted Irish heritage and culture at home and abroad. The works produced in this era were focused on creating a distinctive Irish national theatre, as well as providing plays in English and Irish, though the movement struggled on the stage. This changed when Lady Gregory discovered J. M. Synge, a gifted and natural playwright. However, in 1907 the audience rioted in reaction to Synge's *The Playboy of the Western World*. Gregory telegraphed Yeats: 'Audience broke up in disorder at the word "shift"' – the Irish audience was not prepared to hear about 'good' Irish women in their undergarments. Each night the players continued to perform in dumbshow because of the noise from the rampaging audience until, a week later, Yeats called in the Dublin Metropolitan Police to subdue the rioters (by some accounts, this escalated matters). Throughout all this commotion, the play continued its run and was an economic success. Later that year it toured across the US, where it also caused riots but was largely well received by critics, playing to full houses. Gregory and Yeats considered the tour a triumph. *The Playboy of the Western World* remains one of the primary texts of the Irish Literary Revival.

DID YOU KNOW?

An Taibhdhearc, in Galway, is Ireland's National Irish Language Theatre. They perform famous works translated into Irish as well as original works.

THE ABBEY THEATRE, DUBLIN

Ireland's national theatre was started by Lady Augusta Gregory, Edward Martyn, George Moore and W. B. Yeats in 1899. The Abbey Theatre, home of the Irish National Theatre Society, opened in 1904. Since its inception, its primary focus (which largely remains unchanged today) was to support writers and theatre-makers, while producing works that resonated at home and abroad.

In 1924 Yeats and Gregory offered the Abbey to the Irish Government, who refused, though they decided to give an annual grant to the theatre (then £850) that continues to this day. The Abbey became the first subsidised theatre in the English-speaking world. In 1927 the Abbey opened up 'The Peacock', an experimental space that was also the home of the new Abbey School of Acting. In 1951, the theatre was destroyed by a fire and was relocated to the Queen's Theatre on Pearse Street, returning to Abbey Street in 1966. Since that time, the Abbey has nurtured and premiered works of playwrights including Sean O'Casey, Brian Friel, Marina Carr, Tom Murphy and Mark O'Rowe.

TWENTIETH-CENTURY THEATRE

By the mid-twentieth century, writers were looking to rebel from the familiar tone of nationalism. On a world scale, the art movement was shifting – the time was perfect for Beckett's work to gain notice. Brendan Behan also rose to prominence, offering a kind of anti-hero to the theatre scene. His works focused on Irish culture but he represented a new form of writer: he had grown up in inner-city Dublin, spent time in prison in both England and Ireland (where he learnt Irish and read extensively), and drank heavily.

In the late twentieth century, Irish theatre experienced a surge in companies exploring different styles and methods. There was a lesser emphasis on traditional spaces, broadening the accessibility of theatre throughout the country. Funding increased and artists and writers were exempt from tax, allowing them time to focus and develop their work.

FAMOUS FIGURES
SAMUEL BECKETT (1906–1989)

Samuel Beckett was a minimalist playwright and his works tip over into performance art. His later pieces include poetry, short stories and novellas. His scripts were exacting and he requested in his will that the works should be performed as written. These rules have been relaxed in recent years, allowing for an all-female production of *Waiting for Godot* and a modern-dress production of the same play. When *Godot* premiered in New York in 1956, the advertisers ran a campaign saying: 'Wanted: Intellectuals'. Beckett hated it, as the play was about ordinary people. The work continues to be considered an 'intellectual' play today.

Beckett was notoriously private. Despite Ireland's neutral status during World War Two, he travelled to France and joined the Resistance there. He wrote many of his works in French and later translated them into English. He won the Nobel Prize for Literature in 1968.

DID YOU KNOW?

The Lyric Theatre, Belfast, started in the back rooms of Mary and Pearse O'Malley's house in 1951. Since then, its productions have been performed by some of the most notable theatre actors in the past 50 years, including Adrian Dunbar, Conleth Hill, Ciaran Hinds and Liam Neeson.

FAMOUS FIGURES
CYRIL CUSACK (1910-1993)

Cyril Cusack was born in South Africa to an Irish father and English mother. His parents split when he was young and his mother returned to London, where she worked as a chorus girl. She later moved to Ireland with her partner Breifne O'Rorke. Cyril had his stage debut when he was seven years old. Having joined the Abbey Theatre in

1932, in 1945 he formed his own acting troupe and toured through Ireland and Europe. Throughout the 1950s he had regular film roles in Hollywood and in 1963 he joined the Royal Shakespeare Company. He was nominated for an Oscar for his performance in *My Left Foot*. A prolific actor, he worked right up to the year of his death, aged 82. His six children have all gone on to work in the arts; his daughters – Sinead, Sorcha, Niamh and Catherine – are successful actors of stage and screen, his son Paul is a television director and producer, and Padraig is a theatre producer.

DRUID THEATRE

Druid Theatre was Ireland's first professional theatre company outside of Dublin. Three graduates of NUI Galway – Garry Hynes, Marie Mullen and Mick Lally – founded Druid in 1975. They opened with J. M. Synge's *The Playboy of the Western World*. The company has been extremely successful both in Ireland and abroad, notably at the Edinburgh Fringe Festival and on Broadway. In 1996, they co-produced *The Beauty Queen of Leenane* by Martin McDonagh with the Royal Court in London and the production, which won four Tony Awards, travelled to Sydney and New York. Druid continues to produce new writers and has had a permanent ensemble of actors since 2013.

DID YOU KNOW?

Garry Hynes was the first woman to win a Tony Award for directing.

TWENTY-FIRST-CENTURY THEATRE

In 2010, as part of the economic recovery plan, the majority of Arts Council funding was cut. In a controversial move, the Arts Council cut the funding of certain theatre companies but not others, rather than sharing the loss between the entire community. Many companies were not able to survive the recession, though others tackled their lack of funds creatively. Writers continue to be successful outside of Ireland and many Irish productions have travelled abroad. In more recent years the Arts Council have set up several schemes to decentralise both funding and resources from Dublin and to offer more support to emerging artists.

ART

Ireland isn't well known for its visual art – its artistic prowess lies largely in the hands of its writers – and it can often seem that the highlight of the Irish art scene happened somewhere in the tenth century. There has been significantly more success recently, usually with the work of early twentieth-century artists such as Jack B. Yeats, John Lavery, Roderic O'Conor and Paul Henry. By far the most popular artist is Francis Bacon, who – though born in Ireland where he lived as a teenager – is always classified as a British artist.

Ireland's economic struggles and its history of emigration have not aided the development of art in the country. Catholic conservatism also placed pressure on many of the artists and their desire to push boundaries. One of the few art forms to flourish in Ireland has been the work of stained glass, which benefitted from the approval of the Catholic Church.

However, aside from the lack of historical dexterity, the art scene in Ireland is thriving. Contemporary art is extremely popular: throughout the country, younger artists are receiving funding (though there is much competition) and there are many resources available to aspiring artists.

DID YOU KNOW?

The Hugh Lane Gallery in Dublin was the first public gallery for contemporary art in the British Isles.

FAMOUS FIGURES
JAMES BARRY (1741–1806) – NEOCLASSICAL

In his lifetime James Barry was best known for his difficult personality, though nowadays he is famed as one of Ireland's most influential Neoclassical painters. Unlike his contemporaries, Barry was determined to create art as he saw fit, rather than adhering to the choices of his patrons, and he is considered one of the earliest Romantic painters. Barry began painting at a young age, locally in Cork, and was considered a prodigy. He then travelled through Europe and lived in Italy for nearly three years. He is best known for his six-part series of paintings called *The Progress of Human Culture*, held in the Great Room of the Royal Society of Arts, in London.

DID YOU KNOW?

James Barry was the only artist to be expelled from the Royal Academy of Arts, until Brendan Neil in 2004.

FAMOUS FIGURES
JOHN LAVERY (1856-1941) – IMPRESSIONIST

John Lavery studied at the Haldane Academy in Glasgow and then attended the Académie Julian in Paris. He was one of the members of the 'Glasgow School' who are responsible for many contributions to Art Nouveau and whose work is still visible throughout Glasgow. In 1888, he was commissioned to paint Queen Victoria and soon after moved south to London, becoming a popular portrait artist. He was the official artist of World War One, though he saw little action due to ill health. Lavery was knighted for his contribution to the war in 1918 and elected to the Royal Academy in 1921. During the Irish War of Independence, the Laverys offered their London home to the Irish negotiators. He returned to Ireland, where he continued to work, in the 1930s and died of natural causes in 1941.

DID YOU KNOW?

John Lavery was known as 'the Glasgow boy from Belfast'.

FAMOUS FIGURES
JACK B. YEATS (1871–1957) – EXPRESSIONIST

Jack B. Yeats is one of the best-known and most revered Irish artists. He was the son of the artist John Yeats and brother of the writer W. B. Yeats. Born in London, he grew up mostly in Sligo and considered this place his greatest inspiration. His early work largely comprised illustrations for Cuala Press, run by his sisters Susan and Elizabeth (more commonly called Lily and Lolly), though he is better known for painting day-to-day Irish life and Celtic myths. He fuelled the tide of nationalism after the War of Independence, through his work. Yeats had a unique style and didn't really belong to any specific movement. Initially, he painted in muted tones, but his pieces became more and more abstract – his latest works rarely had lines and were often painted using pallet knives, his fingers and paint straight from the tube.

DID YOU KNOW?

Yeats was the first Irish Free State Olympic medallist. He won silver for his painting, *The Liffey Swim*, in the now defunct arts and culture category of the Olympics.

FAMOUS FIGURES
PAUL HENRY (1877–1958) –
POST-IMPRESSIONIST

Paul Henry was from Belfast but received recognition for his paintings of Achill Island, where he lived for nearly a decade. He trained in Belfast and Paris but returned to Ireland in 1910, living on Achill Island with his first wife, Grace. He moved to Dublin in 1920 and was one of the founding members of the Society of Dublin Painters. Henry began an affair with a young artist, Mabel Young, in 1924 but she left him when she realised he was married. Henry separated from Grace in 1929 and continued the relationship with Young, travelling to exhibitions together. In 1946 Henry lost his sight. He dictated his autobiography to Young who transcribed it for him. Grace died in 1953, and Henry and Young were married the following year.

FAMOUS FIGURES
EILEEN GRAY (1878–1976) – MODERN
MOVEMENT (ARCHITECTURE)

Eileen Gray was born in Enniscorthy, County Wexford, though she was raised between Ireland and London. She was one of the first women accepted into the Slade School of Fine Art. After her training there, she moved to Paris and continued her studies in art, travelling between the French capital, Ireland and London. During this time she became fascinated by lacquer and its techniques. She began learning about decorative lacquer work in London and continued in Paris under the tutelage of Seizo Sugawara.

In 1914 she and Sugawara moved to London because of the outbreak of World War One, returning to Paris towards its end. Gray designed a boutique in Paris from 1917 to 1921, using lacquer on the walls and minimalist modern furniture that she designed, most notably the Bibendum chair. The boutique was a monetary and critical success, giving Gray independence from familial financial support. A few years later one of her lovers, Jean Badovici, convinced her to join him on a project as an architect and designer. The house, E1027, is now a French national culture monument. She continued to design throughout her life, even after her sight and hearing were nearly gone. She lived in Paris until her death at the age of 98.

DID YOU KNOW?

Gray had inherited a peerage title through her mother (the Honourable Lady Gray) that she refused to use.

DID YOU KNOW?

Gray was one of the first women to ever get a driving licence and drove an ambulance in Paris for part of World War One. She also learnt to fly a plane.

FAMOUS FIGURES
SARAH PURSER (1848–1943) – PORTRAITURE

Sarah Purser was an extremely influential artist, though primarily in a social capacity. She was born in Dún Laoghaire, County Dublin, but moved to Dungarvan, County Waterford, when she was very young.

Her art studies began in Dublin and continued later in Paris. She was famously intelligent and popular, and she had an acerbic wit. She enjoyed chatting as she worked, which added to her popularity as a portrait artist, and she made friends with many of her influential clients, such as Maud Gonne, W. B. Yeats, the Gore-Booths and Douglas Hyde.

In 1903 Purser founded An Túr Gloine, a cooperative stained glass studio, so that stained glass could be produced in Ireland, as she strongly believed that the country should produce its own art. She made very wise investments, most notably supporting Guinness, and became very wealthy. She gave back much of her wealth to the arts scene in Ireland, including donating substantial amounts to the Abbey Theatre and the Municipal Gallery of Modern Art.

DID YOU KNOW?

Sarah Purser exhibited as an honorary member of Royal Hibernian Academy (RHA) until 1923, when they finally dropped their ban on women and she became their first female member.

FAMOUS FIGURES
EVIE HONE (1894–1955) – CUBIST

Eva Sydney Hone was a cubist painter and internationally renowned stained glass artist. She trained in London and then travelled with Mainie Jellet to Paris to continue their studies. Upon their return, they held a joint exhibition at the Dublin Painters Gallery, introducing cubism to Ireland, but at first both artists obtained more success in France. Hone began working with stained glass in the 1930s. She worked at An Túr Gloine and later opened her own stained glass studio in Rathfarnham.

DID YOU KNOW?

Evie Hone was very devout – she spent time in an Anglican convent and later, in 1937, converted to Catholicism.

FAMOUS FIGURES
HARRY CLARKE (1889–1931) – ARTS AND CRAFTS MOVEMENT

Henry Patrick Clarke was the son of a church decorator and was apprenticed to him. He studied art in the evenings and then moved to London where he began working as an illustrator. His early commissions were never completed, as they were destroyed in the Easter Rising of 1916. Clarke became an extremely successful illustrator but is most famed for his stained glass work. Having caught tuberculosis in 1929, he travelled to Switzerland for treatment but then, believing he was dying, attempted to return to Ireland and died on the journey. Clarke was buried in Chur. Local law meant that his family had to maintain the grave for the next 15 years, though no one explained this to them so in 1946 he was disinterred and buried in an unknown communal grave.

FAMOUS FIGURES
FRANCIS BACON (1909–1992)

Francis Bacon was a figurative painter and one of the most celebrated artists of his time. He was born in Dublin in 1909 to Australian parents. His mother was the heiress to a steel and coal mine in Sheffield and his father had fought in the Boer War. He had a troubled life: a father who was always uncomfortable with Francis's femininity, abusive relationships with partners and alcohol. The chaos in his life influenced his dysmorphic glamourous style. Growing up, his family moved several times between Ireland and England. In 1926 he was kicked out of his home when his father found him dressing up in his mother's clothes and although he had a small stipend from his trust fund (via his mother), it was not enough to survive so Bacon resorted to avoiding paying rent and petty theft. He floated through several jobs but soon found himself relying on wealthy older men who picked him up in Soho.

After living in Paris, he returned to London around 1929 where he began working as an interior designer and met Eric Hall, who became his patron. Bacon held his first show – furniture and rugs – that winter. He received commissions after this event and began to make a name for himself. His first paintings date from the early 1930s and in 1933 he received some notice for his work *Crucifixion*, though after the ravages of World War One, it was not well received. Throughout World War Two, Bacon continued to paint (he was exempt from service due to his asthma), first in London, where he volunteered for Air Raid Precautions, and then – upon leaving London (due to the dust's effect on his asthma) – in Hampshire.

He returned to the capital in 1943, where he and Hall held roulette parties. In 1945 he was noticed for his work *Three Studies*, which is considered a mark in the post-war art movement. Bacon became successful, moved to Monte Carlo and began gambling. He lost so much money that he couldn't afford new canvases so he would paint on the unprimed side of his previous work – a practice he continued throughout the rest of his career. He returned to London and became a member of the Colony Club, where he brought friends and rich patrons in return for free drinks. He continued to work and socialise until his death in 1992.

DID YOU KNOW?

Bacon's Kensington studio was moved and perfectly reconstructed; it can now be found at the Hugh Lane Gallery in Dublin.

TELEVISION, FILM AND RADIO

TELEVISION – RTÉ

In 1960 the Broadcasting Authority Act removed broadcasting from the direct control of the government and placed it with the newly created Radio Teilifís Éireann Authority (*Teilifís* is the Irish for television and is pronounced 'tel-ih-feesh'; though it is spelt the same, *radio* is pronounced 'rad-ee-o'). In 1961 the new broadcaster, Teilifís Éireann, aired a speech by President de Valera followed by a New Year's Eve concert. In 1978, RTÉ opened up its second channel and in the 1990s it established an independent production unit. Both channels create, produce and buy programmes for broadcast.

DID YOU KNOW?

The Late Late Show, a late night talk show on RTÉ, was first aired in 1962. It is the world's longest running chat show.

FAMOUS FIGURES
GRAHAM LINEHAN (1968–)

One of the most successful TV writers and directors to come out of Ireland is Graham Linehan, who found success with the series *Father Ted*, produced by Hat Trick Productions for Channel 4 in England. Linehan has continued to enjoy success, particularly in comedies including *Black Books*, *The IT Crowd* and a new series, *Motherland*, written with Sharon Horgan (another celebrated Irish comedy writer), which has just been picked up by the BBC. His work has won many awards, including four BAFTAs and an International Emmy.

DID YOU KNOW?

Ireland's first Irish language channel was launched in 1996. It was originally called Teilifís na Gaeilge, or TnaG, though in 1999 it was rebranded as TG4 ('T-G-ka-har').

FILM

The Irish film industry emerged in the 1920s, though it has grown since those early silent films and in the past ten years has flourished to a point that the modern film talent are drawing in line with the traditionally popular fields of theatre and literature. Ireland has a range of production companies of various sizes and, in recent years, a new tax incentive has given the country a competitive edge as a film location.

DID YOU KNOW?

Colm Meaney played the same character three times, though each one with a different name. Three books by Roddy Doyle based on one family – *The Barrytown Trilogy* – were each made into a film by three separate production companies. Having played Mr Rabbitte in *The Commitments*, the name was not allowed to be reused, so he was renamed Larry in *The Van* and Dessie Curley in *The Snapper*.

Ardmore Studios

Ardmore Studios opened in 1958. It was the first film studio in Ireland to offer outdoor locations as well as studio space. The studio was able to draw in large-budget films, which influenced the entire Irish film scene, and is renowned for its ability to transform any area to suit the story – including the hills of Wicklow becoming the Scottish Highlands in Mel Gibson's *Braveheart*, as well as the Ardmore lot transforming into Victorian England in the television series *Penny Dreadful* and sixteenth-century England for *The Tudors*.

Despite its profitability, in late 2016 Ardmore Studios was put up for sale. There was an immediate outcry, including an online petition and a public meeting that was attended by many government officials and important people in the film industry. As 30 per cent of the company is owned by the government, they have the power to veto a sale, which they are unlikely to do unless the new company made significantly less money. At the time of writing there are no guarantees and the successful studios could be resold for development or bought by foreign investors to the detriment of the locals.

Awards

Ireland's films are fast becoming recognised on award circuits and in recent years they have won a plethora of prizes.

ACADEMY AWARDS (OSCARS)	
Best Song	*Once*
Best Short Film	*Six Shooter*
Palme D'Or	*The Wind that Shakes the Barley*
Jury Prize (Cannes)	*The Lobster*
CICAE Prize (Cannes)	*Garage*
Golden Bear (Berlin)	*Bloody Sunday*
Golden Lion (Venice)	*The Magdalene Sisters*

DID YOU KNOW?

The Academy Award statue (Oscar) was designed by Dublin-born art designer Cedric Gibbons. He was also the first Irish person to win an Academy Award, for Best Art Direction for *The Bridge of San Luis Rey*, in 1930. He was nominated 39 times for Best Art Direction and won 11 times.

RADIO

When radio was first introduced to Ireland, radio sets were expensive and rare so people would gather together to listen to important broadcasts. Radio programmes were available from all over the world and this opened up accessibility to new forms of music. Ireland's first radio station, 2RN, was launched in 1926 and renamed Radio Éireann in 1937, consolidating three stations: 2N, 6CK and Radio Athlone. Live commentating on GAA sports has remained one of the most popular transmissions on Irish radio since it was first broadcast. In 1966 Radio Éireann was renamed RTÉ Radio and in 1979 it added its second channel, RTÉ Radio 2, now called 2FM.

DID YOU KNOW?

Ireland was the first country in Europe to broadcast live coverage of a field game. It was the All-Ireland hurling semi-final on 29 August 1926.

SPORT

Sport plays a big role in Ireland, both on a local community level and on a national scale. Ireland is a sports-mad nation, well known for its achievements at an international level. Despite the country's political division, most sports continue to be organised on an all-island basis and remain a force for peace and harmony.

GAA

The Gaelic Athletic Association was set up in 1884 to promote Gaelic games and culture throughout Ireland. It is a national institution – responsible for Gaelic football, hurling, handball and rounders – which works closely with the Camogie Association (Cumann Camogaiochta na nGael) and the Ladies Gaelic Football Association (LGFA). The sports are all amateur at every level and the association is volunteer-led.

HURLING

Hurling is believed to be the world's oldest field game. There are 15 players a side, each with a flat wooden stick, called a *camán* or hurley, and a leather-bound ball called a *sliotar*. The ball can be hit on the ground or in the air and, though it cannot be carried in the hand for more than four steps, it can be balanced on the stick while the player is running or bounced on the hurley and back to the player's hand (this cannot be repeated more than twice). The goalposts are H-shaped, like rugby, with the team receiving a point when the ball goes between the posts above the crossbar and a goal (worth three points) when the ball goes within the posts below the crossbar.

DID YOU KNOW?

Hurling was a demonstration sport at the 1904 Olympics.

FOOTBALL OR GAELIC FOOTBALL

Football is played with a ball that is slightly smaller than an association soccer ball. The ball can be kicked or passed by hand. A player cannot run with the ball further than four steps: they must pass it, bounce it or 'solo' it (dropping the ball onto their foot and kicking it back into their hands as they run). Players are also prohibited from bouncing the ball twice in a row. As with hurling, the goalposts are H-shaped (both games are played on the same pitches), with the team receiving a point when the ball goes between the posts above the crossbar and a goal (worth three points) when the ball goes within the posts below the crossbar.

CAMOGIE

Camogie is the female version of hurling. It has a few differences, including the game being ten minutes shorter, the sliotar slightly smaller and two points being given for a score directly from a sideline cut.

HANDBALL

Handball was one of the original games set out in the GAA charter. There are four types of handball: Four Wall, One Wall, 60 x 30 and Hardball. Four Wall (sometimes called 40 x 20) is the most popular version. It is played indoors and is similar to squash but without a racket. One Wall is growing in popularity and can be played both indoors and outdoors. Sometimes referred to as Softball, 60 x 30 is considered the most traditional version, and Hardball is the fastest version of the sport.

DID YOU KNOW?

Handball is played in North America, Australia, the UK, Spain and Puerto Rico.

ROUNDERS

Rounders was also included in the original charter set out by the Association. The game is similar to baseball, though it is played with a sliotar. Unlike other GAA sports, rounders can be played with mixed teams.

RUGBY

Rugby was introduced to Ireland in the nineteenth century. It became immediately popular and by the 1870s, Ireland was competing internationally. The Union (Irish Rugby Football Union) owns Lansdowne Road where international games are played. It also owns Thomond Park in Limerick, Ravenhill Park in Belfast and various other grounds that are rented to local clubs. Rugby has always been organised on an all-island basis.

FAMOUS FIGURES
BRIAN O'DRISCOLL (1979-)

Now retired, Brian O'Driscoll was one of the most successful Irish rugby players. He played for Leinster and became captain in 2005; he also became captain of the Ireland team (2003–2012), and in 2005 and 2009 he was given the captainship of the Lions. He retired in 2014 and works as a commentator and in various other capacities.

DID YOU KNOW?

Brian O'Driscoll is the highest try scorer in Irish rugby and the second most-capped player in the history of the Rugby Union.

ASSOCIATION FOOTBALL OR SOCCER

Soccer is one of the few sports that are not organised on an all-island basis. The FAI (Football Association of Ireland) was set up in 1921 to organise Association football in the Irish Free State, while the IFA (Irish Football Association) was the organising body for soccer in Northern Ireland. Only Gaelic football has more participants than soccer. Ireland's first international game was in 1926 against Italy. There are two divisions – Premier and First – and the league is made up of several clubs throughout the country. Ireland's national soccer team play on an international level but are probably better known for their fans' devoted and good-natured support than their performances.

DID YOU KNOW?

Prior to the establishment of the FAI, in 1882, Ireland played its first international game against England, losing 13–0.

GOLF

Golf is an extremely popular sport in Ireland: in 1900 there were 72 clubs and today there are over 430. The country's courses are renowned throughout the world and Ireland hosted the Ryder Cup in 2006. After the Republic gained independence, the Golfing Union of Ireland remained united as an organisation representing the entire island.

FAMOUS FIGURES
RORY MCILROY (1989–)

Rory McIlroy is a golfer from County Down in Northern Ireland. He began golfing at a very young age, joining his local club as soon as he was old enough to hold a club. He was the youngest golfer ever to secure his European Tour card. He received his first European title in 2009 at the Dubai Desert Classic, he won his first Major with the US Open in 2011 and the following year he received his second Major (and received two more in 2014). Rory, Jack Nicklaus and Tiger Woods are the only three golfers to have won four Major titles by the age of 25.

CYCLING

Ireland has a long history of competitive cycling. The Irish Champion Bicycle Club – later called the Irish Cycling Association (ICA) – was established in the 1870s and set up the first All-Ireland Cycling Championship in 1877. In 1884 the Gaelic Athletic Association was formed and it also supported cycling as a sport, leading the ICA to fold. In 1922 the GAA began to focus on Irish traditional sports, and the National Athletic and

Cycling Association began (NACA). As the country split, a new organisation was set up in Northern Ireland – the Northern Ireland Amateur Athletic and Cyclists Association (NIAACA) – though the NACA still claimed jurisdiction over the entire island. Over the next few decades, attempts to join these two groups took place several times and an agreement was reached from 1979 to 1988, though this fell through. The divisions were finally overcome in 2007, when both were consolidated into Cycling Ireland.

DID YOU KNOW?

Ireland was the first country outside of France to host the start of the Tour de France. The race travelled through Dundrum in honour of Tour winner Stephen Roche and through Carrick-on-Suir, the hometown of Sean Kelly, in honour of his commitment to cycling and the Tour de France.

MARTIAL ARTS

Martial arts are gaining popularity in Ireland. Sports such as karate, aikido, tae kwon do, kick-boxing and kendo have their own associations, though the increase in mixed martial arts competitions – both at home and abroad – has meant that the broad discipline is more popular than the traditional disciplines.

OLYMPICS

Ireland's Olympic history is a minefield of national pride. Prior to 1906, athletes entered the Olympics independently and Ireland's first Olympic gold medallist, John Pius Boland, won in both singles and doubles (with a German partner) tennis. The Olympics organisers had no Irish flag and Boland was unhappy that the Union Jack was flown when he won. At the 1904 Olympics, Tipperary man Tom Kiely refused funding from both English and American clubs, and raised money locally, determined to represent Ireland.

At the 1906 Athens Olympics three Irish men competed but only discovered upon arrival that the rules had changed so that only National Olympic Committees could nominate competitors. As Ireland did not have a national committee, they were registered as competing for Britain. Peter O'Connor, having won silver, climbed the flagpole in the middle of the medal ceremony to wave his Irish flag (embossed with a harp and the slogan *Erin Go Brach* – 'Ireland forever') in front of the British royalty.

DID YOU KNOW?

John Pius Boland went to Athens as a spectator but took part in the tennis tournament and won gold.

DID YOU KNOW?

Ireland has bid to host the Olympics twice, in 1936 and 1940.

HORSE RACING

Irish people's love of horses and horse racing goes beyond written record. Racing takes place all-year round at 26 racecourses, which host over 350 race meetings with prize money of over €55 million per annum.

EQUESTRIAN SPORTS

Equestrian sport in Ireland covers many disciplines, including dressage, polo, showjumping and carriage driving – to name but a few. The Irish team has had some success in this sport, though it has been shadowed by accusations and proven allegations of drugging.

BOXING

Boxing is a popular sport in Ireland, where the Irish Athletic Boxing Association (IABA) was formed in 1911. John McNally won Ireland's first Olympic medal in the 1952 Olympic Games, coming second. Four years later, in Melbourne, the Irish team took home four medals – and two bronzes followed in Tokyo and Moscow. In 1992, Michael Carruth won Ireland's first Olympic gold medal for boxing. Ireland has continued to bring home medals and is now recognised as one of the best nations for boxing in the world.

DID YOU KNOW?

The IABA is the only amateur boxing association in the world to own and oversee its own stadium.

FAMOUS FIGURES
KATIE TAYLOR (1986-)

Katie Taylor is one of the greatest boxers on the amateur scene and has served as a fantastic ambassador for women's boxing. She has won five World Championships, six European Championships, five European Union Championships and three AIBA World Elite Female Boxer of the Year Awards (2008, 2010 and 2012). She also won a gold medal at the 2012 London Olympics.

DID YOU KNOW?

In the 2012 Olympics the Irish fans broke the records for noise at the Games – they were louder than a jet engine while cheering Katie Taylor on.

CRICKET

While it remains a minority sport, recent successes of both the men's and ladies' One Day International teams have led to an increased participation.

FIELD HOCKEY

This is another all-island sport that is recently undergoing a resurgence.

PORTRAIT OF A PROVINCE: ULSTER

Ulster is the northern province of Ireland. As all of the other provinces, it changed over many centuries but Ulster, as we know it now, began to develop from the time of James I of England and VI of Scotland. Ulster was established in 1219 by John De Courcy and Hugh De Lacy, though at that time it only included Antrim and Down. The Ulster chieftains fought against England during the Nine Years' War and after Elizabeth I defeated the Gaelic lords, the Ulster plantations began, with Protestant English and Scottish farmers being settled into the confiscated lands. Since that time, there has been a battle between Protestants and Catholics for control of the province.

ANTRIM - AONTROIM

Nickname: The Saffron County, Glens County

Song: 'The Green Glens of Antrim'

Antrim means 'lone ridge'. It is home to the Giant's Causeway – a World Heritage Site – and it borders Lough Neagh, the largest lake in Ireland, which feeds the river Bann, the river Lagan and the Lagan Canal. Much of Antrim is very hilly and every October there is a walking festival on the Antrim Hills. Lisburn in Antrim was the centre of the linen industry in Ireland; from its origins in the sixteenth century, this industry went from strength to strength right up to the end of World War Two. Belfast, the capital city of Northern Ireland, is on the east coast, spread across the borders of Antrim and Down.

DID YOU KNOW?

Kenneth Branagh, C. S. Lewis, Van Morrison, James Nesbitt, Georgie Best and Liam Neeson are from County Antrim.

ARMAGH – ÁRD MHACHA

Nickname: Orchard County

Song: 'The Boys from the County Armagh'

Árd Mhacha means 'Macha's height' (Macha was a Celtic goddess). It was home to the settlement of Emain Macha, the real-life equivalent of the mythical setting to many Irish legends. Armagh is called the 'orchard county' because of the amount of orchards and every May the Apple Blossom Festival takes place there. The north of the county borders on Lough Neagh and the majority of the lake's islands are in Armagh's section. Armagh is now mainly Catholic and has always been considered a stronghold of the IRA, though this is contested by many locals as being blown out of proportion by the media.

DID YOU KNOW?

Armagh is the only city in the world that has two cathedrals with the exact same name – they are both called St Patrick's.

CAVAN – CABHÁN

Nickname: Breffni County

Song: 'Come Back Paddy Reilly'

Cavan, like Donegal and Monaghan, is a county in Ulster that is part of the Republic of Ireland. *Cabhán* means 'the hollow', after the land on which the town was built. Cavan is known as Breffni County, named after the tribe that founded the town and ruled the surrounding lands. The source of the Shannon, Ireland's longest river, is in Cavan, which has very fertile lands. Agriculture is still the largest industry in the county.

DID YOU KNOW?

Cavan has a pork festival in Ballyjamesduff which includes a pig race, called the Olympigs, where each pig has a woollen jockey on its back.

DONEGAL – DÚN NA NGALL/TÍR CHONAILL

Nickname: The Tír Conaill Men, Forgotten County

Song: 'Mary from Dungloe'

Dún na nGall means 'fort of foreigners'; the other Irish name for the county, *Tír Chonaill*, means 'the land of Chonaill', after the king of a bygone era. The county is named after Donegal town, though its capital is Lifford and the largest town is Letterkenny. Malin Head, at the very north of the county, is the northernmost point of Ireland. Donegal is the largest county in the province of Ulster and is one of the three Ulster counties in the Republic of Ireland. Donegal has several Irish-speaking areas, including some of the islands off its coast.

TORY ISLAND

Tory Island is off the north-west coast of Donegal. It is a Gaeltacht area named after the Irish translation of *Oileán Thúr Rí* – 'the island of the King's tower'. In Irish legend this island was the home of the Celtic gods, the Fomorians. During the establishment of Christianity, Colmcille founded a monastery on the island, which was the focus point of island life until it was destroyed by Queen Elizabeth I's troops, in 1596. There is a wishing stone on the island that is said to grant your desires if you jump on it or if you can throw four stones that each land on it. The island is the only place in Ireland that is still under the reign of a king, who is elected by the residents (under 100 people). The king's duties include welcoming people to his kingdom and presenting the island's interests to the mainland.

DID YOU KNOW?

Moville in County Donegal holds the biggest Bob Dylan music festival in Europe, every year.

DOWN - DÚN

Nickname: Mourne Country

Down is named after the town of Downpatrick, meaning 'the stronghold of Patrick'. This county town is reported to be the burial place of St Patrick, as well as St Brigid and St Columba. Though Belfast city is in County Antrim, parts of the city spread out into Down, whose largest town is Bangor. Burr Point in the east is the easternmost point of Ireland. Like its neighbour Antrim, Down is one of the only two counties in Ireland that has a majority population of Protestants.

DID YOU KNOW?

Killyleagh Castle is the oldest privately occupied castle in Ireland. It has been a private residence since the twelfth century.

FERMANAGH – FIR MANACH

Nickname: The Lakeland County, Erne County

Fir Manach translates as 'the men of Manach'. Manach is a derivative of Macha, the Celtic goddess of war, horses, sovereignty and women. The county town is Enniskillen, which is also the largest town. Lakes and waterways make up 30 per cent of Fermanagh. Two hills in the Big Dog Forest are called Big Dog and Little Dog – legend has it that the two dogs of Cú Chulainn chased a witch, who transformed them into two hills.

DID YOU KNOW?

Belleek Pottery is from County Fermanagh. The factory has been creating porcelain since 1884.

DERRY/LONDONDERRY – DOIRE

Nickname: Oak Grove County

This county is the only one to have two different names. Doire comes from the Irish word for an oak grove. In 1613 King James I of England and VI of Scotland changed the name to Londonderry. Today both names are used, with Londonderry being preferred by unionists and Derry by nationalists. Mount Sandel in the north of the county is believed to be the earliest settlement within Ireland.

DID YOU KNOW?

The Sperrin Mountains conceal hidden seams of gold; mining began in 2007.

MONAGHAN – MUINEACHÁIN

Nickname: Drumlin County, Farney County

Muineacháin is a term that means 'hills' and also 'bracken'. The county, named after the county town, is the smallest in Ulster and one of the three counties that are part of the province of Ulster but after the Anglo-Irish Treaty became part of the Republic of Ireland. Monaghan was established in 1585 when the Gaelic tribe Mac Mathghamhna signed an allegiance to the British Crown. Later, the Irish earls rose up against the Crown in 1603 but they fled when the rebellion was quashed.

DID YOU KNOW?

Ardal O'Hanlon – the actor best known for playing Father Dougal McGuire in *Father Ted* – is from Monaghan.

TYRONE – TÍR EOGHAIN

Nickname: O'Neill Country, Red Hand County

Tír Eoghain translates as 'the land of Owen', from the ruler Cenél nEógain. Tyrone is the largest county in Northern Ireland, though the land of Cenél nEógain was far greater than the size of the county today. Traditionally, the county was ruled by the O'Neills. In the 1600s the Earl of Tyrone fled during the Flight of the Earls. The county town of Tyrone is Omagh.

FAMOUS FIGURES
BRIAN FRIEL (1929–2015)

Brian Friel hailed from Omagh, County Tyrone. He is best known as a playwright but in later life he was appointed to the Seanad (the upper house of the Irish Parliament). One of the greatest dramatists of his generation, he was celebrated throughout the world for his plays that were considered to represent perfectly the 'voice of Ireland'. He had 24 plays published in just over 50 years and was a member of Aosdána (an association of artists in Ireland that is limited to the top 250 artists of the country) and given the coveted position of Saoi ('wise one'). Only seven Saoi may exist in Aosdána at any one time.

In 1980 he started the Field Day Theatre Company and their first production was his play *Translations*. Over the course of his career, he had considerable international success with: *Philadelphia, Here I come!* (1964), *The Freedom of the City* (1973), *The Faith Healer* (1979), *Translations* (1980) and *Dancing at Lughnasa* (1990). He was a member of many prestigious societies and institutions in

Ireland, the UK and the US, such as the Irish Academy of Letters, the British Royal Society of Literature, and the American Academy of Arts and Letters.

DID YOU KNOW?

Every September the Ulster American Folk Park near Omagh hosts the biggest Appalachian and Blue Grass Music Festival held outside of North America.

SCIENCE AND TECHNOLOGY

Ireland has contributed many breakthroughs in science and technology, though the people behind them often live in the shadow of their sporting and artistic counterparts. Ireland came quite late to the world of science, lacking access to the early academic discourse taking place on the Continent. The sciences in Ireland gained popularity when the University of Dublin, Trinity College, was established in 1592, though an active interest only began to take hold in the late 1600s. Most scientific discovery in Ireland was for practical application up until 1785, when the Royal Irish Academy was established to promote science, polite literature (cultural writings about the arts and belles-letters) and the antiquities. In the nineteenth century the scientific community and its discoveries flourished in Ireland. The popularity of and funding for the sciences declined in the twentieth century until the 1990s, when the government established a commitment to science, technology, research and innovation. The Irish have contributed to the history of inventions – particularly military equipment, including the submarine, the tank, guided missiles and the ejector seat.

PHYSICS

THE BEAUFORT SCALE

Sir Francis Beaufort, from County Meath, created the Beaufort scale in 1805. Beaufort joined the British Navy at the age of 13 and by the time he turned 16, his fascination with the weather was already apparent. He began a journal on weather conditions and he continued to write meteorological journals for the rest of his life. In 1805 he was assigned to a hydrographic survey in South America. He recorded his observations daily, often as frequently as every two hours, and developed a series of abbreviations so he could record quickly and accurately, using a number for wind force (according to a ship's sail) – ranging between 1 (calm) to 13 (hurricane) – and a letter for sky and weather. He developed this system to create his scale which became the official weather notation for all log entries in the British Navy in 1833 and for the Admiralty in 1838. It was edited several times by the International Meteorological Society to adapt it to its new uses, both on steam-powered vessels and on land. In 1947 it was extended to 17 and defined by wind speed. The Beaufort wind speed scale is still used today.

DID YOU KNOW?

The Beaufort Sea in the Arctic Ocean is named after Sir Francis Beaufort.

DID YOU KNOW?

The eccentric Fr Nicholas Callan (1799–1864) was a pioneer in the study of electricity. He created the induction coil and the Maynooth battery. At the time there were no measures for the strength of electricity, so Callan tested currents on his students. After knocking William Walsh (later archbishop of Dublin) unconscious, he was banned from using his students for experiments and began using chickens instead.

FAMOUS FIGURES
DAME JOCELYN BELL BURNELL (1943–)

Dame Susan Jocelyn Bell Burnell was born in Northern Ireland. While studying at Cambridge University, she helped to construct a radio telescope and calculated the observations of distant quasars. During this work she noticed an anomaly in her data that regularly occurred. At first it was brushed aside but Burnell persisted and eventually was able to prove the existence of pulsars. Although her name was second on the paper, Burnell was not included when her supervisor Antony Hewish and astronomer Martin Ryle were awarded the Nobel Prize for Physics in 1974.

CHEMISTRY

FAMOUS FIGURES
ROBERT BOYLE (1627-1691)

Robert Boyle is known as the father of modern chemistry and was a pioneer in the field. Boyle – born in County Waterford in 1627 – was educated at Eton and then continued his studies throughout Europe. Boyle built a laboratory, first in Dorset and later in Oxford, where he could experiment. Prior to Boyle, scientific discoveries were theoretical, argued by the community until they were then tested. Boyle preferred to practise his theories and then draw conclusions. He was the first scientist to perform controlled experiments and then publish the details of the method, apparatus and his interpretation. His experimental studies of the relationship between the pressure and volume of a confined gas led to the formulation, in 1661, of 'Boyle's law' – $p \times V = k$.

THE KELVIN SCALE

William Thomson, a Belfast scientist and inventor, invented the Kelvin temperature scale. The scale uses a unit called a Kelvin and begins at $0°K$, which is absolute zero ($-273°C$) – there are no negative numbers on the scale. The Kelvin scale became popular with scientists, as it was useful for recording very low temperatures, e.g. liquid nitrogen, and because the lack of negative numbers simplified calculations.

BIOLOGY

FAMOUS FIGURES
ELLEN HUTCHINS (1785–1815)

Ellen Hutchins was Ireland's first female botanist. She was born in County Cork and educated in Dublin. While at school, she became sick and after recovering, the doctor advised that she take up a healthy hobby, like botany. Hutchins was particularly interested in plants that do not produce seeds. She collected hundreds of specimens of lichen, mosses, seaweeds and liverworts, and discovered several new species and rare plants. She produced meticulous drawings in watercolour of her findings and corresponded with leading botanists throughout her life, sending them her specimens and drawings (in return for books and information) which were published by the recipients. Letters between them have since established that Hutchins set up this arrangement because she did not want to be published, though she later relented. Many species that she discovered are still named after her.

ASTRONOMY

FAMOUS FIGURES
SIR ROBERT BALL (1840–1913)

Sir Robert Ball was born in Dublin, went to England for secondary education and returned to Ireland to attend Trinity College. He excelled at Trinity and won a scholarship in 1860. Ball took a position as the tutor to the three sons of William Parsons (one of whom was Charles Parsons, see p.240), on the condition that he could use his telescope (in 1845 William Parsons had constructed the largest reflecting telescope in the world at his home in Birr Castle). During this time Ball discovered six previously unknown nebulae. He later became the Royal Astronomer of Ireland and was appointed to the Andrews Chair of Astronomy at Trinity College, Dublin. He wrote several publications on astronomy and was a very popular lecturer in Ireland but he also toured the UK, US and Canada. He was appointed Lowndean Professor of Astronomy and Geometry at Cambridge and was knighted in 1886.

FAMOUS FIGURES
AGNES MARY CLERKE (1842-1907)

Agnes Clerke was born in Skibereen, County Cork. She was educated at home by her parents and showed an interest in astronomy from an early age, completing Herschel's *Outlines of Astronomy* when she was 11 years old. At 15 she began writing her own history of astronomy and at 19 she moved with her family to Dublin where she continued to study the subject, as well as maths and physics. When she was 25, she and her sister Ellen travelled to Italy, where they lived for ten years. While there, Clerke studied science and languages. In 1877, the family were reunited in London and Clerke began to publish her works and was hired to write for the *Encyclopædia Britannica*. She continued to write extensively about astronomy and died while working on the eleventh edition of *Encyclopædia Britannica*.

ENGINEERING

FAMOUS FIGURES
CHARLES PARSONS (1854–1931)

Charles Parsons was born in London and raised in Birr Castle, County Offaly. He is best known for creating the steam turbine. In the midst of the Industrial Revolution, business needed to generate larger amounts of power, and steam engines were proving too large and too loud. Parsons created his first multi-stage reaction turbine in 1884 and quickly set about working on an electrical generator from the converted energy. In 1895 his design was used to power the first electric street lighting in Cambridge. Parsons also worked on marine steam turbines. Using John Wishart's design for a narrow hull and his steam turbine, Parsons designed the ship *Turbania*. While the fastest navy ships of the era could reach only 27 knots, Parsons' new invention reached a speed of 34 knots.

MEDICINE

FAMOUS FIGURES
DR JAMES BARRY (c.1790–1865)

Dr James Barry, born in Cork city in the 1790s, undoubtedly has one of the most interesting biographies in medical history (and possibly in all of history). He performed the second recorded successful Caesarean section and rose through the ranks to hold the highest medical position in the British Army.

In 1865, when Barry's body was being washed and dressed for burial, the charwoman, much to her surprise, discovered that Barry was a woman. James had been born Margaret Bulkley and moved to London with her mother and sister to live with her uncle, the painter James Barry. At her uncle's home she met his patrons: General Francisco Miranda and David Erskine Stuart. When Margaret enrolled at Edinburgh University to study Medicine, she changed her identity, registering as James Miranda Stuart Barry and reducing her age to explain the lack of stubble and high-pitched voice.

After university Barry joined the army as an assistant surgeon and served for 12 years at the Cape Colony, rising to the role of colonial medical inspector. Barry was unpopular in Cape Town, demanding high levels of hygiene (a new fad in medicine), making smallpox inoculations mandatory (20 years before they became compulsory in England), treating all patients equally (including non-white, lepers, as well as those from the asylums and prisons) and insisting on all staff living 'cleanly'. Barry's determination to fight his corner (and his lack of membership to the old boys' club) twice resulted in his demotion but, both times, he worked his way back up the ranks. In 1846 the Duke of Wellington commended his work and soon after Barry was promoted to Inspector General of British Hospitals, the highest rank a doctor could obtain. Once Barry's gender was discovered, the planned military funeral was cancelled and the press was issued a gagging order.

DID YOU KNOW?

Clofazimine, the cure for leprosy, was developed at Trinity College, Dublin, by Dr Vincent Barry (no relation to James) and his team.

THE PORTABLE DEFIBRILLATOR

While working as a professor at Queen's University, Frank Pantridge established a specialist cardiology unit. He and his colleague Dr John Geddes introduced the modern system of CPR, for pre-hospital treatment of cardiac arrest. Pantridge thought this could be improved upon and set about creating a defibrillator that could be kept in an ambulance, as opposed to those larger versions that were available in hospitals. The first portable defibrillator weighed 70 kg and operated from car batteries. It was soon found in ambulances across the globe, though for some reason not the UK, and changed the face of emergency medicine. Nowadays, they are widely available in most public spaces.

DID YOU KNOW?

The binaural stethoscope was created in 1851 by Arthur Leared from County Wexford.

DID YOU KNOW?

Sudocrem was invented by Thomas Smith in 1931. Originally, it was named Smith's Cream and then renamed Soothing Cream, but in 1950 its name changed again, to Sudocrem, because of how it was pronounced in the Dublin accent.

EXPLORATION

Sir Ernest Henry Shackleton was born to Anglo-Irish gentry in County Kildare. He was educated in London and joined the Merchant Navy when he was 16. In 1901 he joined Scott's expedition to reach the South Pole, which was unsuccessful, even though they got closer than any other team had previously. In 1908 Shackleton travelled to the Antarctic again, this time leading the exploration. His team climbed Mount Erebus and made several important scientific discoveries but, once again, he failed to reach the South Pole.

In 1914 Shackleton decided to have one final attempt (though the South Pole had been reached in 1911 by Norwegian explorer Roald Amundsen) and he planned to cross Antarctica, via the South Pole. In 1915 the ship became lodged in ice and ten months later it sank (everyone was already living on the surrounding ice by then). The crew sailed in three small boats, eventually reaching the uninhabitable Elephant Island. Shackleton and five crew members sailed for 16 days in harsh conditions, finally reaching South Georgia. They then trekked across the island until they reached a whaling station and the men on Elephant Island were rescued soon after. Every member of the expedition survived.

MATHEMATICS

William Hamilton was born in Dublin and was a prodigy. He knew 13 languages by the time he was nine years old. Hamilton became Professor of Astronomy at Trinity College and Royal Astronomer of Ireland. He introduced the terms 'scalar' and 'vector' into mathematics, and he invented the method of quaternions as a new algebraic approach to 3D geometry. This turned out to be the seed of much of modern algebra.

BOOLEAN ALGEBRA

Born in Lincolnshire, in England, George Boole was a self-taught mathematician and his publications were so impressive that he was appointed the first Professor of Mathematics at Queen's College, Cork, despite not having a university degree. While there, he developed his system of Boolean algebra, which has laid the foundations for the science of electronic computers and much of the electric hardware responsible for modern technology.

FOOD

Ireland has long been considered at the bottom of the food scale but in recent years there has been a resurgence in native cuisine and a growing appreciation for the country's products. With the economic boom of the Celtic Tiger and increased popularity of travel, the Irish began to cultivate finer palates. There is a new generation of artisan producers, across all of the food and drink industries, whose products are being used to create dishes of a global standard by locals, small businesses and Michelin-starred chefs.

The Irish have three main meals a day:

	breakfast
lunch (in cities)	dinner (in rural areas)
dinner (in cities)	supper (in rural areas)

Traditionally, the largest main meal was in the afternoon, in order to provide the most energy in the fields, and was followed by a snack in the evening, but this practice is largely dying out, as the modern system of an evening meal has become more popular.

> ## DID YOU KNOW?
>
> Irish custom requires that you turn down the offer of generosity, though the correct response to that is for the offer to be repeated. If someone refuses your offer to pay for dinner, you should offer at least three more times before they'll definitely allow you to pay – sure, it'd be rude not to!

Takeaway dinners are now very popular in Ireland. Pizza, Chinese food, and fish and chips have been staples for many years, while Thai, West African and Eastern European cuisines are growing in popularity. However, the surge in takeaway dining has led to obesity problems. The country is considering a 'fast-food tax' and there are many school and television campaigns aimed at tackling the health of the country.

> ## DID YOU KNOW?
>
> In Northern Ireland fish and chips is known as a 'fish supper'.

POPULAR BRANDS

AVONMORE MILK
Milk is a staple of the Irish diet. There are lots of small dairies across Ireland but the most popular brand is Avonmore.

Originated in County Kilkenny in the 1960s, the company merged with Waterford Foods and created Glanbia plc. Avonmore milk is run by 'Avonmore Creameries Federation', a cooperative of 36 smaller societies each made up of small dairies.

BRENNANS BREAD

Bread is another staple in the Irish diet. The most popular type sold in Ireland is Brennans sliced pan, which originated in The Liberties, an area in central Dublin. It is still a family-run company and the bread is still wrapped in wax paper, unlike that of many rivals that have switched to plastic. Brennans make their products through the night so that fresh bread is on the supermarket shelves each morning, throughout the country.

DID YOU KNOW?

Brennans were the first company to wrap their bread in wax paper.

CADBURY DAIRY MILK

Dairy Milk is the most popular chocolate bar in Ireland. It is a simple milk chocolate bar with eight squares and made from the traditional Cadbury recipe (that uses a 'glass and a half of milk' – that's 426 ml to every 227 g of chocolate). It is produced in Dublin: although Cadbury is a British company, they opened an Irish factory in 1933 to combat de Valera's high taxes on imported goods. There are many chocolate bars that are only available in Ireland, such as Caramello, Mint Crisp and Golden Crisp, which are variants of the Dairy Milk.

GUINNESS

Guinness is a popular stout across the world and the favourite alcoholic beverage in Ireland. The brewery was set up in 1759 in Dublin by Arthur Guinness and is now owned by Diageo. The stout is mixed with nitrogen and carbon dioxide as it's poured, which give it its characteristic thick creamy head. It is also why the drink needs time to 'settle' after it is poured.

DID YOU KNOW?

The ancient Irish harp was first used to represent Guinness and only later became the national symbol of Ireland.

JACOB'S KIMBERLEY BISCUITS

Jacob's Biscuits was established in 1851 – its Kimberley biscuits (a sandwich biscuit with mallow in the middle) are Ireland's most popular biscuits and one of the top ten items sold in Irish supermarkets. Personally, I prefer a chocolate Kimberley, but the original ones are synonymous with Irish childhood.

JAMESON WHISKEY

Jameson is the most popular Irish whiskey in Ireland and in the world. The company was established in 1810, though it is now owned by Irish Distillers as part of Pernod Ricard. It is distilled in Cork and its ingredients are sourced from within Ireland.

DID YOU KNOW?

Whiskey from Ireland has an 'e' in it. Whisky without the 'e' is from Scotland.

TAYTO

Tayto are Ireland's most popular crisps. There are two Tayto companies: the first was established in the Republic in 1956 and, as it grew in popularity, a new one – that licensed the branding and recipes from the original company – opened with the same name in Northern Ireland. Tayto crisps (in the Republic) were the first company to use a flavoured crisp production process. They are a cultural institution and expats, from both sides of the border, are particular about having 'their' Tayto.

POPULAR CHEESES

Ireland, with all of its rain, produces great dairy products, and cheeses are a particular highlight. There are many types and varieties – some of the most popular and most celebrated cheeses have been listed in this section.

ARDRAHAN

In 1983 Eugene and Mary Burns started making cheese using traditional methods on their farm in County Cork. They now make two cheeses – Ardrahan and Duhallow – which have won many awards over the years.

CASHEL BLUE

After she attended a cheese making course, Jane Grubb began to make lots of different cheeses from her and her husband Louis's dairy farm, selling them in local markets. In 1984 she created Cashel Blue, which was their first blue cheese. It was an immediate success and was served to Elizabeth II on her state visit to Ireland in 2012.

CHEDDAR

Cheddar is the most popular type of cheese in Ireland. There are many different brands, as Cheddar is mass produced and readily available in every supermarket, but Ireland also has some local producers that create finer quality types, such as Coolattin, Mount Callan and Bay Lough Cheddars.

DURRUS

Another Cork cheese, Durrus, began production in 1979 – again, made from traditional methods. The cheese is semi-soft and becomes stronger in taste (and smell) with age. It has won many awards at home and abroad.

FISH

Until recently meat was never eaten on a Friday, as it was against the Catholic religion. Nowadays, people rarely pay attention to this, though some will still abstain from meat on Good Friday (commemorating the crucifixion of Jesus). Since fish was connected to fast days, it became associated with poverty and remains less eaten in Ireland than most island nations. Shellfish, in particular, were considered a pauper's food, though they are now becoming far more popular. Dublin Bay prawns (langoustines), oysters, clams and mussels are all regularly available in supermarkets and in restaurants. Seaweed, however, has always been popular, particularly in the north and west of the island. Carrageen, often referred to as Irish Moss, is the most widespread. Cod and salmon are the most popular fish. Most of the latter is farmed, though wild salmon is still available (and unbeatable for taste). Smoked salmon is an Irish specialty: usually oak-smoked (though any wood or turf can be used), it is filleted and hung in a smokehouse for a long time.

DRINKS

POITÍN

Poitín means 'little pot' and gets its name because of how it was (and is) distilled. It was most commonly a home-made alcohol produced from potatoes (though it can be made from cereals, grain, whey, sugar beet and molasses as well). In 1556, the law changed to require a licence to distil spirits, though poitín continued to be made at home. In 1661 it was declared illegal and soon its production became a small and popular act of minor rebellion. Part of its notoriety came from the lack of control over alcohol content, meaning that each bottle was a gamble. It was legalised in 1997 and has a minimum alcohol strength of 40 per cent but can go as high as 90 per cent. Since 2015, poitín has a 'technical file' from the Department of Agriculture that sets out the parameters of what can be called 'Irish poitín', including that it must be made within Ireland (North or Republic). The primary difference between poitín and whiskey is that the former is not aged.

DID YOU KNOW?

In order to be classified as 'Irish poitín', over 50 per cent of the ingredients must be sourced in Ireland.

RED LEMONADE

Red lemonade is a popular drink in Ireland, though there is no consensus on where it originated or why it has never spread to other parts of the world. The drink, which became popular in the nineteenth century, is fizzy and lemon flavoured, although it has other flavourings that vary between brands. It has always been popular with children and some believe its staying power (compared to that of its clear, pink and cloudy cousins) is partly due to how popular it is as a pairing with Ireland's other favourite drink: whiskey.

DID YOU KNOW?

Fizzy non-alcoholic drinks are called 'minerals' in Ireland. The most popular is Coca-Cola.

HOT WHISKEY

A hot whiskey is made by adding together a generous shot of whiskey, a little sugar and some cloves stuck into a lemon (so they don't float in the glass), topped with hot water. It is the go-to cure for a cold.

> ## DID YOU KNOW?
>
> A hot whiskey is often confused with a hot toddy. A hot toddy originates from the UK and, although often virtually identical, it is usually made with honey rather than sugar and has further additions, such as herbs, tea and/or spices.

HOT PORT

Hot port, in essence, is Ireland's answer to a mulled wine, but it's far easier and quicker to make. Like a hot whiskey, it comprises a shot of port, some brown sugar, a lime or lemon wedge (I prefer lime) studded with cloves and hot water to top it up. It is very popular at Christmas time, though it is not linked to the festivities – it's simply a good winter drink.

IRISH COFFEE

There are many theories related to when Irish coffee was created. It is likely that versions of the drink (cocktails of whiskey and coffee) existed from the nineteenth century but the drink as it is known today probably originated in 1940s Limerick. The drink comprises a shot of whiskey with a little sugar (less than a teaspoon) added to warm coffee and with cream poured on top.

> ## DID YOU KNOW?
>
> Nowadays, the phrase 'to make it Irish' means adding whiskey to... well, frankly anything.

DID YOU KNOW?

The Irish drink more tea per capita than anywhere else in the world.

BRANDED DRINKS

GUNPOWDER GIN

Drumshanbo Gunpowder Irish Gin (to give it its full name) comes from The Shed Distillery in County Leitrim. It is a mixture of oriental botanicals (including gunpowder tea, which gives its name to the gin) and Irish ones. It is hand distilled using traditional methods and medieval copper pot stills.

METALMAN BREWING

Metalman Brewing is a small brewery in County Waterford. It makes a range of beers and is steadily growing. It produces around 20 different beers; some of these are available all year round, while others are short releases. The company is named after a – rather dapper – maritime beacon (a figure dressed in British sailors' uniform, standing on a tall pillar as a warning of the dangerous cliffs) near Newtown Cove, Co. Waterford, which was erected in 1823.

O'HARA'S IRISH STOUT

O'Hara's is a traditional stout from Carlow Brewing Company. This small craft beer company started in 1996 and is still family-owned. It brews several different beers but is best known for its stout, which began production in 1999. The stout has won several awards, most notably the Millennium International Brewing Industry Awards in 2000.

DID YOU KNOW?

Black and Tan (stout and ale) and Belfast Bombers (a shot of Baileys and brandy dropped into a half-pint of Guinness) are never ordered by the Irish. They're still considered quite offensive.

DISTILLERIES

Ireland has many distilleries across the country and as the craft market gains popularity, more and more are opening up.

TEELING
The Teeling Distillery makes several different whiskeys and was the first new distillery to open in Dublin for 125 years. It is located in The Liberties and is the only active distillery that remains in the city. The current owners of Teeling are descended from a family of distillers – their ancestor Walter Teeling opened his distillery in 1782.

> ## DID YOU KNOW?
>
> Whiskey must be aged in wooden casks for no less than three years in order to officially be sold as 'whiskey'.

BLACKWATER DISTILLERY

Blackwater Distillery, in County Waterford, was the first craft gin distillery in Ireland. They now make poitín and whiskey, as well as five types of gin. Each of their products is made in small batches in their little distillery using traditional methods and Irish produce.

TRADITIONAL DISHES

BACON AND CABBAGE

Bacon and cabbage is the most popular dish in Ireland according to a survey by Aramark Ireland (a global food services and facilities company). It is a traditional dish that is still made at home. Irish bacon, which is cured (unlike its North American counterpart), is often boiled (with an onion to soak up the salt) and then baked. The cabbage, on the other hand, can be boiled or fried. Often the bacon, potatoes and cabbage were all boiled together.

BARMBRACK

Barmbrack is a form of fruit cake, or tea cake, which is traditionally served at Hallowe'en with different items in it. Nowadays, it tends to contain a ring and whoever finds it will be the next to marry, though there used to be various items representing different futures (some much better than others).

> *Pea – you'll be poor.*
> *Coin – you'll be rich.*
> *Stick – you'll be beaten.*

BLAA

The blaa is a soft fluffy white-bread bun with a floury crust particular to County Waterford. They are best eaten fresh, as they do not have a long shelf life. Although they have been a staple in Waterford for centuries, blaas have grown in popularity across the country only recently and they are often enjoyed with rashers (slices of bacon) in the morning, especially after a night out.

DID YOU KNOW?

The term 'Waterford blaa' is protected: it can only be used to describe blaas made within the county and by certain bakeries that have official permission.

BOXTY

There are three types of boxty, named after how they are cooked. Pan boxty is a form of potato pancake made from (last night's) mashed potato and grated raw potato, mixed together with flour, eggs and milk, and then fried in butter. It can also be mixed without the milk and egg, and then sliced and fried. Loaf boxty is the same dish, though baked in the oven, and boiled boxty is – you guessed it – boiled (almost like a dumpling) and then fried in a pan.

An Irish rhyme:

> *Boxty on the griddle,*
> *Boxty in the pan,*
> *If you can't make boxty,*
> *You'll never get a man.*

BROWN BREAD

Irish brown bread is a soda bread made partly with wholemeal flour, rather than entirely white (and without dried fruit, which the white has). It is a non-yeast bread, using baking soda instead.

GRANNY MEADE'S BROWN BREAD RECIPE

Partly because this remains my favourite brown bread (and mostly because I don't have to apply for rights to reprint it), here is my granny's recipe for traditional brown bread. It looks American but she used an actual teacup, not the US measurement. Also, she didn't actually measure the ingredients – just threw it into a bowl – so this is an approximation (same for the instructions, e.g. heat of the oven). Good luck!

Serves 5

INGREDIENTS

4 cups wholemeal flour (coarse wholemeal works best)

1 cup white flour

1 tsp salt

2 tsp bread soda (sodium bicarbonate)

2 tsp sugar

2 oz butter

Sour milk (preferably) or buttermilk

PREPARATION METHOD

Preheat oven to 200–230°C.

Put all the dry ingredients in a bowl and mix.

Rub in the butter.

Mix with the milk. Do not have it too dry or the bread will be hard but not too wet either – just soft.

Turn out onto a floured board and knead lightly, just enough to shape into a round.

Put on a baking sheet. Mark with a deep cross.

Bake in a hot oven for 40–45 minutes.

Once baked (knock on the bottom to check!), place on a wire rack.

CHAMP

Mashed potato – adding butter and milk (and cream if you're lucky) – with chopped spring onions. It originated from Northern Ireland and the name comes from the Scots term for ground (or food) that has been macerated. It would have been eaten as an entire meal, though now it is a side dish.

CODDLE

This is a Dublin meal. It is a form of stew which uses the leftovers of the week and some sausages, and slowly leaves them to simmer (or coddle). It was traditionally served with soda bread. It was always considered a dish of the poor of Dublin.

COLCANNON

Mashed potato, as with champ, but with kale or cabbage instead of spring onions. Outside of Ireland people add meat or fry the dish – although admittedly very tasty, technically this isn't really colcannon. Colcannon has always been a vegetable dish.

CRUBEENS

Boiled pigs' feet (never had it, never want to). They are often battered and then fried, though sometimes they are wrapped in bacon and fried. James Joyce mentions crubeens in his most famous novel, *Ulysses*. They used to be sold as street food and bar food (great for making the punters thirsty), but they have gone out of fashion in modern Ireland.

FADGE

Fadge is a potato bread that is found in Northern Ireland. A little like brown bread, it is made from a mix of potato flour and white flour. Potato farl, as found in an Ulster Fry, is a slice of this bread. Regionally, the bread has several names, including slims, tatie bread, tawty, and so on.

THE FULL IRISH AND THE ULSTER FRY

A full Irish is eaten in the Republic and an Ulster Fry is the same meal but with the added extra of potato farl. They are both derived from the traditional English fry-up.

Within a Fry there are:

- ❖ Sausages – usually pork sausages with high bread content

- ❖ Rashers – thin strips of bacon

- ❖ Black pudding – pork fat, pork blood and oats (honestly, it's better than it sounds)

- ❖ White pudding – like black pudding, but without the blood

- ❖ Eggs – usually fried, though sometimes they're scrambled

- ❖ Potato farl – a bread made with potato flour

Also popular are sautéed mushrooms, fried tomato, hash browns, liver, baked beans, soda bread, boxty or toast.

SODA BREAD
Soda bread, in Ireland, refers to a sweet white bread that has dried fruit in it. The bread is made with soft flour, buttermilk and bread soda (which react together to create the air that makes the dough rise) rather than yeast and strong flour like most types of bread. It is also not kneaded.

STEW
Irish stew is a staple dish that is very simple. It can be made with any meat, although it was traditionally made with mutton. The meat is braised, the onions fried, and then potatoes and other root vegetables are added – as well as water, stock and herbs – and boiled (for a long, long time).

SELECTED BIBLIOGRAPHY

Boylan, Ciara *The Little Book of Ireland* (2nd edn, 2013, The History Press)

Broderick, Marian *Wild Irish Women: Extraordinary Lives from History* (6th edn, 2001, O'Brien Press)

Burke, Fatti and John *Irelandopedia* (2015, Gill & MacMillan)

Burke, Fatti and John *Historopedia* (2016, Gill & MacMillan)

Cronin, Mike, Duncan, Mark and Rouse, Paul *The GAA: A People's History* (2009, Collins Press)

Evans, Bruce and Power, Martine *Lonely Planet; Irish Language and Culture* (2013, Lonely Planet)

Gallagher, Tara, Biggs, Fiona and O'Duibhir, Fionnbarra *A Pocket History of the 1916 Rising: The Story of Ireland's Independence* (2015, Gill Books)

Hoad, T. F. *The Concise Oxford History of English Etymology* (1993, Oxford University Press)

Mabey, Richard *The Cabaret of Plants* (2015, Profile Books)

Mac Uistin, Liam *The Tain* (6th edn, 1989, O'Brien Press)

McDonald, Ferdie *Eyewitness Travel, Ireland* (20th edn, 1995, Penguin Random House)

McQuillan, Neil, Griffin, Brendon, Rawes, Olivia and Mills, Rachel *The Rough Guide to Ireland* (11th edn, 1986, Rough Guides/Penguin Random House)

Moody, T. W. and Martin, F. X. *The Course of Irish History* (19th edn, 1967, Mercier Press)

Morash, Christopher *A History of Irish Theatre 1601-2000* (2nd edn, 2002, Cambridge University Press)

Plehov, Mel and Golding, Elizabeth *The Pocket Encyclopedia of Ireland* (2nd edn, 2012, Gill Books)

Reynolds, Mark, McCoy, Niamh, McKeigue, Julianne and Clarke, Joanne *The Pocket Book of the GAA* (2016, Gill Books)

Williams, Mark *Ireland's Immortals; A History of the Gods of Irish Myth* (2016, Princeton University Press)

ACKNOWLEDGEMENTS

A massive thank you to Abbie Headon for all your support and wise words, Debbie Chapman for all your help and Daniela Nava for your incredible accuracy (and patience). So many thank-yous to the incredibly wonderful Daly – there simply aren't enough words for your brilliance and if there were, you'd use them against me. HTHF I have been doing a lot of research, working on accuracy and fact, so, as ye know, I am better with each one of you in my life and so incredibly grateful for each and every moment. Mammy Meade, putter-upper of no nonsense and Daddy Meade president of the world: thank you both for your support, encouragement and practical advice (and a very special thank you Dad for your time and effort – you went so far beyond proofreading, this book would be nothing without your input). Thanks to Emer for all her love and support and most importantly the fun. Adrian Brannigan, thank you for your fantastic drinks knowledge, and for introducing me to Gunpowder Gin and Blackwater Gin – hell, thanks for the info, tasters and cocktails! Nick, Marcus, Mon, Sheila and Jess – sure, ye couldn't handle an egg! But thanks for putting up with me as I wrote this. Niall, Vivienne, Adrienne and Geraldine – I can only presume this is how the nightly prayer went before I was born.

Obviously, things are so much better now… Thank you for your advice and support and kindness. Thank you to Henry Martin and Francis Turnley, whose advice has been invaluable. You are inspirational, and I don't say that lightly. Jackie, Lucy and Renée – thanks for being fun, intelligent, artistic, wise brilliant women who made this book a better product.

Though some of ye have already been mentioned, thanks to my readers (and offerers of reading, who are just as important): Dad, John Carroll, Sheila Kelly, Jennifer Carroll, Ciara Daly, Natalie Pool, Naomi Moran, Lucy Smith, Geraldine Meade, Adrienne Meade, Liane Escorza and Caroline O'Sullivan.

Thanks to Virgin Lounge, Côte Marylebone and Marylebone Library – this book would never have happened (and I mean that) if I couldn't have run to you during my lunchbreaks.

IRELAND

The Land of a Hundred Thousand Welcomes

Clare Gallagher

IRELAND
The Land of a Hundred Thousand Welcomes

Clare Gallagher

ISBN: 978-1-84953-520-5

Hardback
£5.99

'We may have bad weather in Ireland,
but the sun shines in the hearts of the
people and that keeps us all warm.'

Anonymous

Enjoy this leprechaun-sized guide to all that's best about the Emerald Isle, from myths and legends to must-see places to visit, interspersed with hilarious one-liners, jokes and plenty of Irish charm.

IN PRAISE OF
IRELAND

IN PRAISE OF IRELAND

Paul Harper

ISBN: 978-1-84953-561-8

Hardback
£5.99

Ireland's beautiful landscapes and rich histories have long moved great writers and poets to capture their glory.

Ranging from timeless prose to lyrical poetry, from incisive wit to thoughtful social commentary, these stirring volumes collect the most inspiring praise for our beloved countries.

If you're interested in finding out more about our books,
find us on Facebook at **Summersdale Publishers** and
follow us on Twitter at **@Summersdale**.

www.summersdale.com

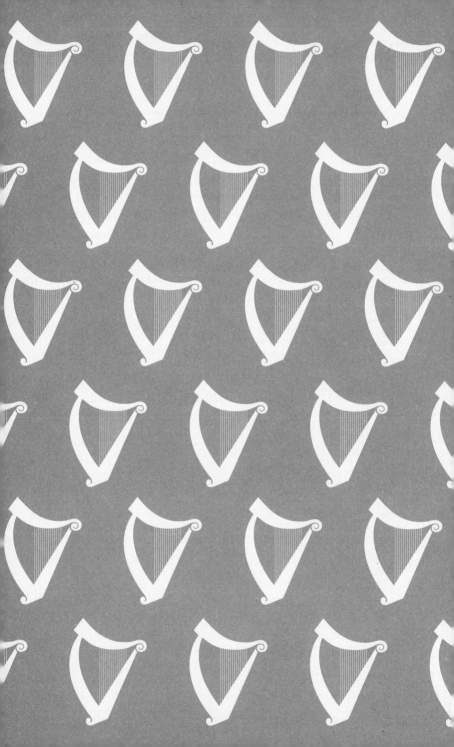